Caring for
EXOTIC
BIRDS

Caring for
EXOTIC
BIRDS

Marcus Schneck and Jill Caravan

CHARTWELL
BOOKS, INC.

A QUINTET BOOK

Published by Chartwell Books
A Division of Book Sales, Inc.
110 Enterprise Avenue
Secaucus, New Jersey 07094

ISBN 1-55521-730-3

This book was designed and produced by
Quintet Publishing Limited
6 Blundell Street
London N7 9BH

Creative Director: Terry Jeavons
Designer: Michael Morey
Project Editor: Lindsay Porter
Editor: Rosemary Booton
Picture Researchers: Marcus Schneck and
Jill Caravan
Illustrator: Danny McBride

Typeset in Great Britain by
Central Southern Typesetters, Eastbourne
Manufactured in Hong Kong by
Regent Publishing Services Limited
Printed in Singapore by
Star Standard Industries Pte. Ltd.

CONTENTS

INTRODUCTION

Birds were among the very first animals that man domesticated to his use, probably right on the heels of the dog. Domestic chickens date back to the first permanent human settlement in India, about 5,000 years ago. And, even before early man had settled fully into stationary communities, nomadic peoples were using falcons and other raptors as a means of hunting.

Exotic birds, with their ornamental, rather than utilitarian, appeal were originally the province of the great civilizations. Evidence suggests that Egyptian rulers and nobility collected and caged colourful African birds as early as 4000 BC. The pursuit at that time involved incredible expense and so remained a hobby only for the very wealthy.

With the rise of the Greek Empire, this civilization too came to cherish exotic birds as a symbol of status, power and wealth. Shortly before his death in 323 BC, Alexander the Great brought dozens, possibly hundreds, of parrots and peafowl back from his last great conquests in India. He even extended his royal protection to all peafowl in all lands under his domain.

The Renaissance in Europe (AD 1300–1600), as part of the explosion of knowledge and enlightenment that resulted when the stagnant stranglehold of the Church was finally broken, brought about a boom in garden aviaries among the wealthy classes across the Continent.

The exploration of the New World brought a previously unknown array of exotic birds to the growing ranks of bird fanciers. One of the discoveries that Columbus brought back to Queen Isabella from his first voyage was a pair of Cuban Amazon parrots. He reported that the native peoples of the island kept several species of domesticated parrots and parakeets as pets.

Long before this first European contact it was common throughout the Inca Empire for homes to have several tamed parrots flitting about. The feathers of certain birds were part of the tribute that the Inca rulers demanded of inland tribes under their domination.

Gradually, as exploration continued and transportation evolved to accommodate more varied cargo, exotic birds became available to ever larger numbers of people. The first bird shows were held in England in the 1890s. Because of the bird diseases that soon spread as a result of this close contact, an interest in bird health and nutrition also began to flourish at about that time.

Getting started

The magnificent colours, the wonderful intelligence in their eyes, the intriguing ability to fly, the possibility of specialized tricks, such as 'talking', all combine to give exotic birds a unique appeal. But the prospective owner must also be fully aware of the unique responsibility that comes with bird ownership. The provision of special diet and environment and the danger of disease are all part of that responsibility.

ABOVE Sooner or later you may experience an outdoor escape by your bird. Generally, gentle pursuit combined with offerings of treats will retrieve the escapee.

OPPOSITE The more freedom that birds can be given, the better off they will be, both physically and mentally. In the wild they lead relatively active lives.

In some species, such as the African grey parrot, that responsibility might extend over the 60 or 70 years of the bird's life. Even the tiny canary may very well be a member of the household for the next 10 to 20 years.

These same factors can just as easily be seen as positive reasons for entering the world of aviculture. They are presented here in their starkest forms to enable the new bird owner to enter the pursuit with his or her eyes wide open.

Finches, canaries, cockatiels and budgerigars are the usual starting-point for new bird fanciers. They are available at relatively low cost, and the care they need – while every bit as necessary – is easy when compared with that of the large parrots and macaws. These smaller, 'easier' birds are often purchased as pets for children. They can open a child's eyes to the wonders of nature. Nevertheless a careful and honest assessment of the child's ability to take on even these relatively limited responsibilities must be made before any purchase is considered. General experience shows that the parent usually assumes most of the responsibility for any pet after the initial novelty wears off for the child. Add to this the fact that birds are not the cuddliest of pets.

Again, the worst-case scenarios are presented here in the hope that any new bird owner is prepared for the implications of the experience that he or she has chosen to undertake. The purpose

TOP Whenever possible, the cage bird's life will be greatly enhanced if more than one can be purchased and housed together. Contact is an important part of daily life to many species.

ABOVE Children are generally inquisitive about birds, and vice versa. However, both parties in the encounter have the potential to injure the other.

LEFT Some children take the responsibilities of bird ownership very seriously. Others, however, soon lose interest in a new pet that can't be cuddled, leaving the care and nurturing of the bird to their parents.

bird to stretch to its full wingspan without touching the sides of the enclosure, to fly from perch to perch without obstruction, and to perch without touching the top with its head or the sides or floor with its tail. The cage should be sturdy, and should contain horizontal bars to facilitate climbing.

The cage should be placed away from areas of sudden temperature change and away from all

is not to discourage interest in the hobby, but neither is it to over-glorify. A balanced, natural approach is always the best course when dealing with living things.

In addition to the responsibility that comes with a bird, the prospective owner must consider many other factors when planning a purchase.

Space considerations are crucial. Large parrots need very roomy cages and 'playground' areas. Even the tiny finches must have sufficient space for flight. An incredible selection of cages awaits the buyer upon entering any pet shop or opening the pages of any pet supply catalogue. Cages range from the traditional metal-barred type to vitrines, which are glass-enclosed showcases that have regained popularity in recent years. There are also many wooden models, which are quite serviceable for some small species. However, the chewing habits and abilities of many of the larger birds make wood a poor choice for them. Remember that composite wood should never be used in any bird construction because of the fumes that this chemically treated material emits.

Whatever selection is made, a comfortable environment must allow enough room for the

LEFT Metal cages are an absolute must for the larger birds, such as the macaws, because they will explore and challenge every inch of their cages on a regular basis. Any weak spot could lead to a break-out.

gases, fumes and other odours, including tobacco smoke and cooking smells. Also, it should be placed away from any television set, as high frequencies that cannot be heard by human beings can damage a bird's nervous system. A cage must be easy to clean and maintain, with a floor of wire mesh that allows droppings to pass through onto a removable tray. All-metal cages are easiest to wash with soap and water, and to disinfect.

The bottom of the cage should be lined with paper, as other materials tend to lead to problems of their own. Food and water dishes should be plastic, ceramic or stainless steel, and must be removed for daily cleaning. Additional, shallow

BELOW Feeding bowls that encourage the bird to perch on the bowl while feeding can be wasteful of food. Some food is usually lost when the bird lands and takes off from the bowl.

ABOVE An incredible array of cage designs and sizes awaits the buyer at any well-stocked pet shop.

OPPOSITE The macaws are large, powerful and noisy birds that the novice aviculturalist will find difficult to enjoy.

containers holding both water and sand should be provided for the bird's bathing.

A separate area, such as a small wooden breeding box, must be attached to the cage to enable the bird to enjoy daily periods of privacy. An exercise area must provide activity facilities similar to those the bird would enjoy in the wild (see *Bird Care* p23).

Plan to clean all droppings from the cage at least once a day and clean the entire cage at least once a week. Wash all surfaces with soap and hot water, being certain to remove any debris so the disinfectant can kill all viruses, spores and

RIGHT When kept outdoors birds enjoy the sun, but they must also have adequate shade to escape rays during the hottest part of the day.

BELOW This pair of African grey parrots has been provided with ample flight space in their outdoor aviary. However, their lives would be enhanced by a few more perches and objects to interest them.

bacteria. Chlorine bleach at a strength of 1 fluid ounce to 1½ pints (1 fl oz to 1 US quart/28 ml to 0.9 l) of water makes a suitable disinfectant. All cage objects should be soaked in this solution for 30 minutes and then thoroughly rinsed.

Another possibility, for those who have the necessary space, is an outdoor aviary. At its most basic, the aviary includes a large, outdoor flight area and a connecting shelter. It might also include a birdroom, with indoor flight areas for winter use, and breeding cages. Several considerations must go into the siting decision, including weather, sun position, enjoyment of your birds, their comfort, planning restrictions, neighbours, and possible intruders. For example, in temperate regions it is not feasible for birds to remain outdoors throughout the entire year.

To make the extra work of an outdoor enclosure worthwhile, the aviary should be no less than 10 feet (3m) in length and no less than three feet (1m) in width. However, the more space you can give your birds the more comfortable they will be. Concrete provides the easiest cleaning, most disease-resistant floor surface. Living plants, which greatly enhance any aviary, can be provided in pots. Some plants which are suitable for the aviary include bamboo, blackberry, clematis,

When a species has been selected, the new owner's next step is consideration of individual birds. Health factors are critical. Definite signals of a potentially troubled bird are listed in the table above).

ABOVE If space permits, birds of several species can be kept together in the same cage or aviary. However, all residents should be of relatively the same size.

RIGHT Any reputable bird dealer or pet shop will allow a check-up by a veterinary surgeon of your choice before you buy a bird.

elderberry, holly, honeysuckle, jasmine, morning glory, nasturtium, pyracantha, rhododendron, silver fir and snowberry. Proper ventilation is essential for the birdroom to prevent diseases and an ionizer will improve the air quality even further. All these environmental necessities should be installed and operational before any bird is purchased.

Next, consider the temperament and habits of the species you are acquiring. (These aspects are covered in general in the listings in the second half of the book.) Pet-shop owners, breeders, veterinary surgeons, zookeepers and bird owners can all offer valuable insights into the species with which they are familiar.

ABOVE Several large parrots await auction in a group holding area.

Remember you are making an investment and commitment that could very well last many years, so study the bird carefully. Reputable dealers will allow a check-up of the bird by a veterinary surgeon prior to the sale, and a few hours of observation before the purchase is not at all unreasonable.

An increasingly important aspect of any exotic bird is the animal's place of origin. As you'll see in the individual listings later in the book, many species are now considered endangered and threatened in the wild. Buying any bird that has been removed from the wild carries implications that must be seriously considered.

More than 85 per cent of all parrot species have now been bred and reared under captive conditions. Captive-bred birds represent no net loss from the wild and, if they are bought for further breeding, actually may mean a net gain for the species' overall, worldwide population. In addition, they generally have not undergone the extremely stressful and lengthy ordeal of birds taken from the wild, even of those that arrive through legal channels.

In addition, the World Wide Fund for Nature estimates that at least 225,000 birds worth more than £30 million ($50 million) are smuggled or imported with forged documents into the US each year. These smuggling methods can involve everything from binding birds into hubcaps to placing them in hollowed watermelons. Nearly 80 of the world's 330 parrot species are in danger of extinction in the wild because of this illegal trade.

RIGHT This red-headed parrot has been dyed yellow by a smuggler to increase its value as a cage bird. Its life has probably been shortened by the action.

Purchase of any illegally imported birds carries many dangers for the buyer. These birds have not been through the normal quarantine procedures and they can carry diseases that threaten both other birds and human beings. And, it is common practice for smugglers to disguise low-quality birds with dyes, paints and physical alterations to make them look like species that fetch a much greater price.

Leg banding is the principal means of identifying the origination of a bird. A seamless leg band is a solid ring of metal that is attached to the leg of a newly hatched live bird and cannot be removed, once the bird has reached adult size, without destroying the band (see illustration p15). These bands are attached to captive-born birds. By contrast, open-ring leg bands are applied to the legs of live wild birds of any age, using pliers or similar tools.

Acclimatization

With the quarters established and the specific bird selected, it is time to introduce the new member of the family to its new home. Stress is a primary contributor to sickness and disease in birds and this introduction period is potentially very stressful. You should do everything you can to make this time as pleasant and stress-free as possible for the bird.

Make sure you have the same food mixture that the pet shop or breeder was feeding the bird waiting for it in its new cage. If necessary, you can gradually change the bird over to a better

METHOD OF RINGING A CHICK

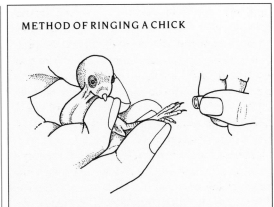

1 With the first finger and thumb of the hand in which the bird is held, gather the three long toes together, holding them in position by the ball of the foot.

2 Pick up the ring and slide it over these toes, then pass it over the ball of the foot, gradually sliding it up the leg.

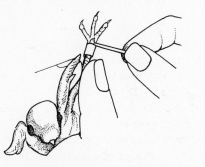

3 To release the short back toe, which is now held against the leg by the ring, insert a pointed stick, such as a matchstick, between the toe and leg and gently ease the toe through the ring.

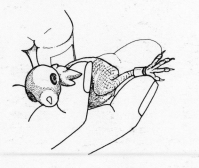

4 The ring is now correctly positioned around the chick's leg.

diet when it has settled comfortably into its new environment. If it refuses to eat, which is not at all uncommon at this point, offer it some honey in small amounts. Few birds can resist honey and it helps to stimulate the digestive systems of nearly all creatures.

Keep disturbances near the cage to a minimum. No bird should ever be greeted by a crowd of onlookers upon arrival. Force yourself to resist the temptation, give the bird several days to get comfortable with its new surroundings and then gradually introduce it to other people and pets.

Taming and training

The first step towards turning your new bird into a family pet must be getting acquainted. To do this, try to see the world through the bird's eyes: it's frightened, alone and in a totally foreign

ABOVE Most cage birds can be trained to perch on their owner's fingers. Every effort should be made to teach the bird that this is in fact a pleasurable experience.

environment. To reassure the bird of its safety, move very slowly and talk gently. Several days may pass before it begins to calm down. Take advantage of this time to familiarize yourself with the bird's signals, both through its 'speech' and through its body language.

When the bird begins to tolerate your presence close to the cage without becoming overly agitated, you are ready to begin training it to the hand. No matter how frustrated you may become during the next phase of training, you must at all times demonstrate the overall enjoyment that the bird can feel by perching on your hand. No session should last more than 15 minutes, which is about the maximum attention/patience span for a bird.

Never hit a bird to discipline it, no matter what it may do. Birds simply do not have the capacity to accept force as anything other than a

HAND-TRAINING

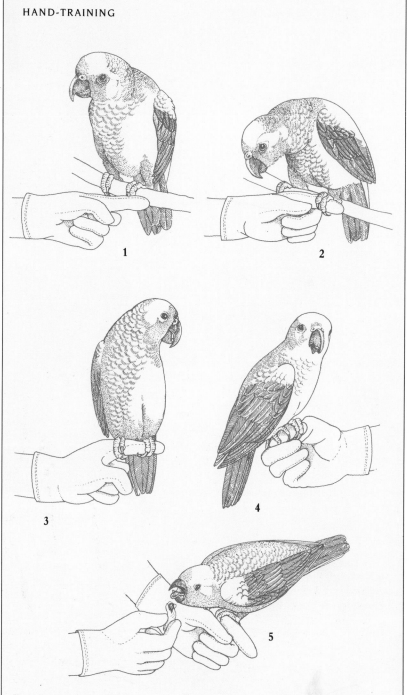

PERCHING

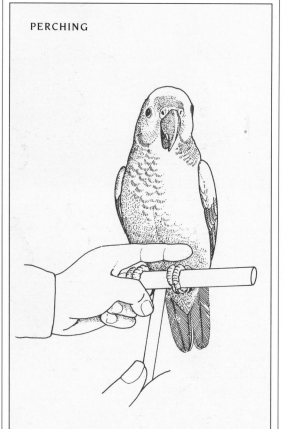

To train your pet bird to perch on your finger, move the index finger against the abdomen just above the legs. Press softly and carefully. The bird will usually oblige by seating itself on the finger.

1–3 Hand-taming a bird is not difficult, if the bird is young. First it must be persuaded to adopt the hand as an alternative perch. A glove may be necessary in the early stages, particularly if the bird's claws are sharp.

4–5 Once the bird is perching readily on the finger, it can be fed with the other hand, thus reinforcing the bond with the owner. The length of time taken to reach this stage will vary. Ideally, two or three short

training sessions should be carried out every day. Hand-raised birds will be most receptive to such training.

threat. Patience and gentleness are the only things to which they will respond. For your own safety, wear leather gloves to work with medium-sized birds, such as the smaller parrots, and hold a stick for the cockatoos and macaws.

Begin the process with your hand inside the cage, where the bird has come to feel relatively secure. Moving very slowly and talking gently to the bird, softly push your hand or stick against the bird where its chest and legs meets. This will usually force the bird to jump onto your finger or stick. With the larger birds repeat this procedure several times each day for at least a week with the stick and then begin again using your flattened hand.

After at least a week of success inside the cage, begin offering the bird small treats with your free hand whenever it perches on your other hand. When the bird has become totally at ease with this phase, slowly pull your hand with the bird on it out of the cage. The first few times that you do this, the bird will probably jump off your hand or try to grab the bars when it nears the door. Be patient and continue the process until the bird is relaxed on your hand outside the cage.

If, when it is outside the cage, the bird flies off your hand, don't make a grab for it. Allow it to fly about the room, which should have been completely sealed off before beginning the work, and then slowly approach with your perching hand extended to the bird. If it will not respond, try holding a treat over the perching hand. If this fails, allow the bird to rest for a while and then try again.

Only now can a second person be brought into the room. Begin the process again from day one, inside the cage at first, with the new person close to the cage. Gradually move through the whole process and eventually allow the additional person to present a few treats to the bird as it perches on your hand outside the cage.

Repetition is the key to training a bird to do anything, and that includes 'talking'. All members of the parrot family, from the budgerigars to the macaws, are capable of imitating human speech, as well as many other sounds. Slowly and gently repeat the desired word over and over again to the bird. No lesson should last more than 15 minutes, but remember also to repeat the word whenever you pass the cage. Bird-training tapes are available that may help in this process, but there is no substitute for hard work on your part.

ABOVE Treats must be an integral part of all training sessions, which should be limited to no more than 15 minutes at a time.

BELOW Human-bird relationships, if carefully built and nurtured, will be filled with tender moments equal to those possible with any other type of pet.

ABOVE The back of the neck is an important social-contact spot among birds. This can be incorporated into human-bird relationships as well.

LEFT A scratch behind the head is welcomed by most birds, once they have grown comfortable in the relationship with their owner.

RIGHT Birds should be discouraged from biting the hand that holds them. However, no bird will respond to being hit. Verbal reprimands and gentle pushing of the bird's head away from the biting spot will prove much more effective.

When the bird makes its first word, lavish treats upon it along with any particular praise to which it has shown a liking. Each new word after this first one will probably come more quickly and easily.

This procedure will work for the many different tricks that owners teach their birds to perform. The easiest actions to teach them will be those that emulate and build on actions they already do on their own in their cages when they are undisturbed; such as climbing, carrying small objects and flying from one perch to another.

Bird diet

Each of the listings in the second half of the book provides detailed information about the diets of the individual species; however, there are some general considerations for any feeding programme.

First of all, the bird owner must be aware that birds eat an incredible amount of food by human standards. Some of the smallest species eat as much as twice their own weight every day.

Birds also appreciate and thrive on as much variety as possible in their diet; however, the basis of every diet should be a properly formulated pellet. Several manufacturers produce varieties of these pellets designed for different species. Some birds, particularly those that have been conditioned to eating seeds only, may need to be 'converted' to pellets in their diet. To do this, only pellets should be offered for a few days, followed by a half-and-half mixture of pellets and seeds for a few days, followed by just pellets again for a few days. The process should be continued until the bird is accustomed to eating pellets as its sole meal.

While modern pellets provide for the bird's full nutritional requirements, variety is essential for a bird to lead a happy, fulfilled life. The pellets should be supplemented regularly with seeds and nuts, fresh vegetables, fresh fruits, protein (meat, poultry, fish, eggs, legumes, and insects) and very small amounts of dairy produce such as

RIGHT Teaching tricks to birds requires a great deal of patience and repetition. Tricks that build upon the natural antics of the specific bird come easiest.

yoghurt and cheese. Fresh vegetables may make up as much as 45 per cent of the diet for some species and fresh fruit may contribute 20 per cent, but too much of either of these will lead to loose droppings. Important vegetables are dandelion, cress, spinach and carrots. Avoid large amounts of lettuce, which can lead to gastrointestinal problems, and never serve cabbage. All vegetables should be served at room temperature, never straight from the refrigerator, to avoid severe chills to the bird's digestive system.

Where weather permits and birds are kept outside or in outdoor birdrooms during the winter, extra protein should be offered in addition

to some starches. These will give the birds more body fat to withstand the cold.

Cuttlefish bones, oyster shells and commercial mineral blocks should be offered as additional sources of important minerals. Vitamin and mineral supplements are also advisable when birds exhibit signs of illness.

Clean, fresh water must be kept available to the bird at all times, both as a source for drinking and for bathing. Use only bottled water, or tap water that has been boiled to remove any impurities.

Bird physiology

Feathers are the most instantly notable feature of any bird's physique. In addition to their flight-enabling features, they are also one of every bird's primary defences against cold temperatures. All birds can fluff their feathers to create insulating air pockets next to their bodies. For this reason fluffing can often be taken as an early sign of illness, as the bird tries to fight off a chill. Feathers also serve their owners in territorial, courtship and mating matters. Further, they often provide a portion of the bird's nesting materials. There are three types of feathers:

CONTOUR FEATHERS These are the main plumage of the body, wings and tail. Each contour feather features a long quill with interlocking

OPPOSITE Greens should be offered as a regular part of the bird's diet, although pellets should be the keystone on which the diet is built.

OPPOSITE BELOW Cuttlefish bone is an important element of any bird cage. It provides exercise, stimulation and necessary minerals.

BELOW Shallow water sources are necessary to avoid drowned birds, who love to bathe.

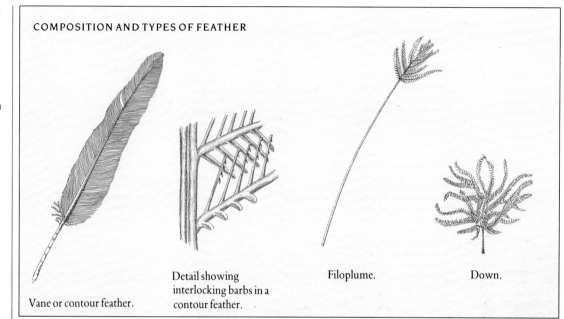

COMPOSITION AND TYPES OF FEATHER

Vane or contour feather.

Detail showing interlocking barbs in a contour feather.

Filoplume.

Down.

regular touching of the beak to the preen gland at the base of the tail. This gland produces an oil that is essential to the maintenance of the feathers. But even with this constant attention, feathers do wear out and must be replaced regularly. Moulting is the natural, cyclical replacement of old, worn feathers, and failure to moult is a definite signal of illness.

Feather colour is mostly the result of pigments in the feathers and the way light reflects off the feathers. Reds, oranges and yellows are generally barbs. Flight feathers are specialized versions of contour feathers.

FILIOPLUMES These are hairlike, with thin quills and fluffy tufts at their tips.

DOWN Down is made up of the very fluffy, almost furlike feathers that occur under the contour feathers in adults and comprise almost all the plumage of very young birds. Down feathers provide insulation.

Beneath all these feathers, the bird's skin is relatively thin. Therefore, the birds have to rely instead on their outer, feathery coating for protection from the elements.

Bird's spend a great deal of time preening their feathers. Part of this frequent ritual includes

BELOW A close-up of a macaw's wing shows the intricate, interlocking pattern of the bird's feathers.

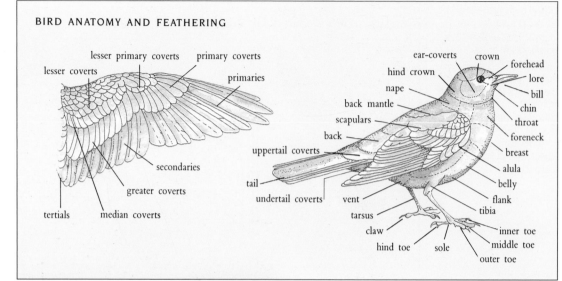

BIRD ANATOMY AND FEATHERING

lesser coverts
lesser primary coverts
primary coverts
primaries
secondaries
greater coverts
median coverts
tertials
tail
uppertail coverts
undertail coverts
back
scapulars
back mantle
nape
hind crown
ear-coverts
crown
forehead
lore
bill
chin
throat
foreneck
breast
alula
belly
flank
tibia
vent
tarsus
claw
hind toe
sole
inner toe
middle toe
outer toe

BELOW The beak is an important 'third foot' for many of the climbing birds, such as the various macaws.

caused by carotenoid pigments; blacks and browns by melanins; and blue principally by light. Mutations of the normal plumage colour patterns for any given species of bird result when the genes that normally provide the code for those patterns are modified. Most colour mutations in the wild tend to die out with the specimen that received them, unless they somehow enhance that individual's chances of survival. Under domesticated conditions, however, desired mutations can be nurtured and protected. Selective breeding programmes can actually be used to develop the mutations further.

The same evolutionary process that permits birds to fly has left some evidence of the bird's reptilian ancestors in the scales on the legs and feet. These scales provide armour-like protection to the limbs. Toes and claws, on the other hand, have evolved to meet the specific lifestyles of their owners. The perching birds, such as the canaries and finches, sport feet with three toes pointing forwards and one pointing backwards, each equipped with a thin and sharp claw. The feet of the climbers, the psittacines, have two toes pointing forwards and two pointing backwards, each with a thick and curved claw.

Evolution has also made substantial changes inside the bird to enable flight. Many bones have air spaces and hollows that lessen the bird's overall weight, while also providing additional storage space for the massive amounts of oxygen that flight requires. The respiratory system is very efficient for this same reason, and also to cope with the relatively high metabolic rate of

RIGHT When the bird is allowed to explore a room without restraint, all plants should be removed or at least checked to determine if they could be poisonous to the bird.

the avian world. Larger birds, such as cockatoos and macaws, draw and process about 30 to 40 breaths per minute, while small birds, such as the canaries, take about 100 breaths per minute. By contrast, the average adult human being breaths 15 to 25 times a minute.

Digestion, too, is very swift in birds. Fruit eaters digest and eliminate food such as berries within 30 minutes of first swallowing them. Seed and nut eaters generally take about three hours to achieve total digestion. This, of course, means that birds defecate many times every day: 25 to 50 times every 24 hours is normal.

The bird's beak, of course, is not very much involved in the process of digestion. It will be used to grasp a food item, and possibly to crack nuts or seeds and separate the edible kernel from the chaff. But, without teeth, most of the grinding and disintegrating of food items into usable nutrition is accomplished in the bird's gizzard, a very large and very strong stomach where food items are gound up with the help of grit.

Bird care

Daily exercise periods are necessary to maintain the bird's health, and these should allow for all activities that the bird would engage in when living in the wild.

In addition to adequate flight space within its enclosure, the bird should be allowed some free flight outside the cage. A room of the house, most likely the one in which the bird is regularly housed in its cage, will serve this function well. All poisonous plants should be removed; mirrors, windows and anything else that the bird might decide to fly 'through' or attack because of a

BELOW T-perches allow much-needed time outside the cage to birds that have had their wings clipped.

ABOVE Wooden perches are essential to the well-being, both physical and mental, of most birds. They provide for both exercise and mental stimulation as one additional distraction in the environment.

reflection should be covered; lock the doors to prevent unexpected escape routes. Do everything to provide the bird with a secure and serene atmosphere, and leave the cage door open for voluntary returns.

The bird's legs and feet are kept in tone by perching and climbing activities. A range of perch sizes – oval not round – provides for the variation needed to use these different muscles. The perches should be widely spaced, and positioned in an uneven arrangement. Larger parrots should be given T-perches outside their cages, but they should not be chained to these perches. With easy access to food and water, the parrots will generally be content to perch on these structures for long periods at a time.

The growth of the bird's beak is continuous throughout its life. It must be worn down constantly through cracking seeds and nuts, rubbing on branches, grasping to climb, and other activities. Chewing on wood is thus a favourite activity for many birds. Cuttlefish bones and lava stones also fulfil this need, providing crucial minerals at the same time.

Mental exercise is just as important. Birds need games and toys, sights and sounds to remain physically sharp. T-perches and tree branches,

Birds also are generally pretty good at giving
signals as to their physical health. The many ill-
nesses, diseases, injuries and parasites that can be
suffered by birds would fill a book many times
the size of this volume; however, the following
behavioural changes can be taken as general

BELOW Mirrors
provide welcome
stimulation for the smaller
cage birds. The larger
species, however, will
damage the mirror.

especially when outside the cage, help larger
parrots to keep in top form, as playful and responsive pets. Large wooden objects (soft, dry
wood), rawhide and large bells are other useful
stimuli. Smaller birds enjoy small versions of all
of these things, as well as mirrors, ladders and
(sometimes) swings.

Above all, birds thrive mentally on companionship. For the solitary pet, this means time
every day with its owner. Companionship aids,
such as tape recordings, will help give the bird a
mental work-out, but nothing replaces that
regular time together.

Birds have many ways of telling us if they are
not getting enough mental stimulation. All of
the activities listed in the table above are warning
signals.

SYMPTOMS OF AN UNHEALTHY BIRD

- Appetite change
- Increased thirst
- Change in colour or consistency of droppings
- Inactivity
- Fluffed feathers
- Overly extended moulting period
- Picking and scratching at feathers
- Change in voice
- Sneezing or coughing
- Erratic and repeated body or tail movements
- Sitting on the cage floor for long periods
- Discharges from any body openings

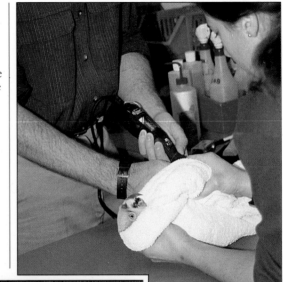

RIGHT A visit to the veterinary surgeon may be a good idea for the bird's first nail-clipping. Watch carefully how the vet handles the bird and clips the nails so that you can emulate the procedure the next time, if you want.

indicators that something is amiss. When you think your bird is ill, provide a warm environment (about 90°F/32.5°C), make food and water easily available, and consult with your veterinary surgeon. The early warning signals are listed in the table above.

Grooming

If you've provided your bird with an adequate variety of sizes of perches and climbing areas, normal activity will generally keep its nails worn down. However, nail length should be checked regularly. Should the nails grow too long they could cause the bird to have difficulty in standing or perching. The tips of the forward-pointing claws should not meet or overlap those of the backward-pointing toes.

If necessary, trimming can be done with fingernail clippers or, for larger parrots, with dog nail clippers. The cut should be made just in front of the pink area, which contains blood vessels and nerves. A torch shone through the nail will help identify this dermal region, which you should not cut into. Any bleeding that does occur should be stopped as soon as possible with a styptic pencil or powder, or with direct pressure. If it can't be stopped quickly, consult your vet. Even a seemingly tiny amount of blood can be a lot to a small bird.

Like nails, the bird's beak should be kept to a desirable length through normal day-to-day wear. However, if it grows so long as to interfere with the birds eating, it must be cut. The procedure is similar to that for nails.

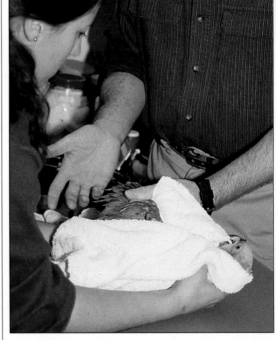

LEFT Wing clipping requires a practised eye and touch. Feathers can bleed, leading to complications, if they are cut incorrectly.

In both instances, many owners feel much more secure in asking their veterinary surgeon to do the cutting, at least the first few times.

Wing trimming is done for a very different reason: to prevent the bird from flying. The most popular and attractive method is to cut most of the primary flight feathers and secondaries close to the body. Bleeding is a distinct possibility if a blood feather – distinguished by its blue quill – is cut. If that does occur, the entire feather must be removed. The veterinary surgeon definitely should be called on to perform this task the first few times, until you feel confident.

RIGHT After they have become comfortable in their new home, birds thrive on contact. If that contact is not with other birds, it must come from their human owners.

BELOW A completely enclosed nest box will enhance breeding success, as it allows for a calm parent bird throughout the period.

Breeding

Only a small number of bird owners ever venture into the fascinating but frustrating area of breeding their pets, and only a small proportion of these actually make a serious attempt at it.

The best start for a serious breeding programme is with the purchase of several birds of the desired species, which are then allowed to develop pairs among themselves. This is more expensive than chancing on one selected pair, but it is probably the quickest route to success.

Once a mated pair has emerged from the initial group, the other birds should be moved to other quarters. They can be kept in reserve should one of the mated pair die, or for mating with offspring of the original pair.

Different species will have different requirements in terms of nesting sites and nest materials, and these must be met to continue on the path to success. Many of these pecularities are covered in the individual species discussions later on. A number of species, however, have adapted well to breeding cages, among them canaries, finches and budgerigars. Breeding cages of the correct dimensions and design are available commercially for these and other birds.

The one thing that all birds have in common in the breeding and nesting season is the need for surroundings that are as calm and undisturbed as possible. Slow and quiet approaches to the cage or aviary should be the rule. Even the most gentle approach may elicit a reaction from the birds at this time. Many species, particularly the larger parrots, become very aggressive during the breeding season.

You may look in the nest or nest box whenever both parents are out. However, you will be very likely to cause damaged eggs or injured chicks if you do this when either parent is in.

With nesting conditions satisfied, and climatic and daylight factors telling the birds that the season is right, it may not be all that long before the first egg appears in the nest. At this point the bird, especially if she is in her first nesting season, may appear rather reluctant to become a parent. However, her reluctance to stay on the nest does not usually present a problem as the egg will remain viable for several days, and the bird will probably become much more interested in her nest on the laying of the second egg.

Most breeders at one time or another will encounter eggs that just do not hatch. There are many reasons for this, including the fact that the egg was never fertilized, or the chick died inside the egg.

With the hatching of the chicks, the food needs of the parent birds will escalate. As they are now eating for more than one bird, additional protein is especially welcome in their diet at this time.

ABOVE Disturbances should be kept to a minimum throughout the breeding and rearing period, but particularly when eggs or young birds could be damaged by excited parents.

BELOW Feather growth has begun on this pair of nestling parakeets, shown inside the nest box.

In some species chicks naturally undergo a small loss of weight just before fledging. A slight loss is nothing to be alarmed about; however, substantial and rapid weight loss – especially if accompanied by a listless manner and ruffled feathers – is cause for calling on a vet.

A careful and frequent check on the young birds must be maintained from this point until they are fledged from the nest. At any time, particularly when they begin to show feathers, the parents may become quite neglectful. If the babies' crops have a slack look to them, especially at night when they should be stuffed, and if their growth rates appear to be stunted, it may be time to take them from the nest and begin the process of hand-rearing.

The chicks must now be kept at about 100°F (38.1°C). They will give you signals if the temperature is uncomfortable: if it's too cold they will huddle together for warmth; if it's too hot they will separate and hold their wings away from their bodies. Plastic cups lined with tissue are a perfect environment for the tiny birds at this point, each bird should be in its own cup, with its own feeding equipment. This separation will help prevent the spread of any infection that might arise.

An incredible array of quite satisfactory feeding mixtures is available commercially. Whichever you select, for the first few days it must be very liquid when served. Serve it warm, never hot,

with a small spoon or dropper, and clean any excess off the beak immediately after feeding. Until they reach about seven days of age, the young birds will need to be fed at least every two hours. After their first week, this can be reduced gradually to about four-hour intervals. At all times, it is much better for the young birds to be fed smaller amounts frequently, on demand rather than larger amounts less often.

The crop is a good indicator of when to feed and how much food to give each bird. At the completion of the feeding session, the crop should appear relatively full. When it looks slack, it's time for the next feed. If it never looks slack, there is probably something amiss. Consult a veterinary surgeon immediately.

Gradually the feeding mixture can be made less liquid and enhanced with finely ground sunflower seeds, vitamin and mineral supplements, and powdered cuttlefish bone.

Maintain detailed records of everything you do and the exact results all through the rearing period. Very little is known about proper methods for many exotic species, and amateur breeders can help to advance substantially aviculture knowledge in this area.

After the breeding and rearing period, all containers and tools, such as feeding droppers, spoons, nesting box and breeding cage, should be cleaned thoroughly with soap and water, and then disinfected. Otherwise, these surfaces and structures offer prime locations for the spread of bacteria and parasites.

Using this book

In the following pages many of the most popular cage-bird species are discussed in detail. A few pheasant and quail species, and the blue peafowl, have also been covered to present the full range of possibilities to the new aviculturalist.

Although the status of each bird in the wild is clearly indicated, as rainforest destruction continues worldwide, the status of these birds will become increasingly tenuous.

BELOW Few private owners can allot this amount of space to their birds. But imagine the full lives that these macaws must lead.

DIRECTORY
OF
BIRDS

Using the directory

The following symbols are used in the directory to represent the habits of individual species:

DIET

insect-eaters

fruit-eaters

seed-eaters

SOCIABILITY

birds which thrive in a solitary environment

birds which thrive in pairs

birds which are happiest living in a group.

VOICE

birds which sing a great deal. When only the male of the species sings, or when singing occurs only during a particular season (ie breeding), this symbol has not been included.

birds which can be taught to speak. The introduction includes details on training.

STATUS

The status of each species described is in accordance with the listings established by the Convention on International Trade in Endangered Species of Wild Flora and Fauna (CITES). The following categories have been established:

Appendix 1. These birds are the most highly endangered and are therefore given the highest level of protection under CITES. Commercial trade in any of these species, when taken from the wild, is banned, and permits are required from both the country of export and the country of import for any trade whatsoever.

Appendix 2. There is some concern about the survival of these species in the wild. Some limits are placed on trade, with permits required from the country of export.

Appendix 3. This is a special listing by a particular country that believes the species listed needs some monitoring. Export permits are required.

BELOW The Toco toucan is a popular species with aviculturists. The status of the bird in the wild is not yet under threat.

LEFT Although the Moloccun cockatoo is a good-natured pet, the space essential to its well-being may not be available to all.

BELOW The red lory will be more content if kept in pairs.

RIGHT A multi-bird environment will provide much more insight into the lives of the birds than a lone bird can ever provide.

Ringneck Parakeet

INDIAN RINGNECK, ROSE-FRINGED PARAKEET

Psittacula krameri manillensis
ORDER Psittaciformes FAMILY Psittacidae

DESCRIPTION 16 inches (41cm). Green, with black collar, beak band and stripe between nostrils and eyes. Red shine behind collar. Yellowish-green belly and undertail coverts, bluish-green tail feathers with yellow tips. Eyes yellow-orange, beak red, legs black. Immatures resemble adult hen, but have greenish irises and paler bills. Well-known mutations include lutino (sex-linked); blue (autosomal recessive); albino (formed from lutino and blue); cinnamon (or isabelle); grey (dominant when paired to normal).

Species may have been known to Alexander the Great (356–323 BC). The related, but larger, Alexandrine Parakeet (*P. eupatria*) in fact bears his name. Apart from variation in size, only plumage distinction is that Alexandrines also have red shoulder patches.

NATURAL DISTRIBUTION Covers wider area than any other species of psittacine, from north-west Africa through Asia as far east as Burma, and into China. Introduced to many other localities.

HABITAT Gardens, parks, farmland, woodland and timbered areas and lowland of Sri Lanka. Sometimes in flocks of about 15,000. Likes to bathe in the rain. Flocks split up during breeding season, each pair nesting in a tree cavity after courtship ritual: female twitters and rolls eyes at strutting male, rubs bills with him and accepts food. Even so, no firm pair bonding. Female dominates.

DIET Ripening fruit, grain (will even invade grainstores, opening sacks with hooked bills and squabbling over spoils), parrot mixture, greenstuff and non-fatty seeds.

SPECIAL NEEDS Generous aviary, 12 to 16 feet (4 to 5m) long, because reportedly males in small areas become sterile. Young independent birds should be placed in roomy flight. Tolerates light frost, but provide temperate, protected area.

CAGE LIFE Ideal aviary pet, may talk well and can live for more than half a century. Possible to keep colonies. Lays 3 to 6 white eggs, incubation 22 to 26 days by female, fledging 45 to 52 days. Female starts nest inspection early in the year and will build the nest in about three days. She chews the wood shavings and chips placed in the nest box (10 × 10 × 16 inches/25 × 25 × 40cm, entrance diameter 3 inches/8cm) into shape. Male feeds both female and chicks; hen helps feed after a week.

STATUS IN WILD Appendix 3.

Ringneck parakeet

Plum-headed parakeet

Plum-Headed Parakeet

Psittacula cyanocephala
ORDER Psittaciformes FAMILY Psittacidae

DESCRIPTION 13½ to 15 inches (33 to 37.5cm). Male green with plum-coloured head, black neck ring, bluish-green band on nape, brown-red shoulder spot. Inner tail bluish-green, outer green with pale yellow tips. Eyes brown, beak yellowish-white, legs greyish-brown. In the hen red shoulder marks missing, neck band lighter and greyish-purple. Young birds reach adult colours after two years, young males resemble females.

NATURAL DISTRIBUTION India, western Pakistan, Nepal, Bhutan, west Bengal and Sri Lanka, in two subspecies.

HABITAT Jungles, cultivated areas, forests at elevations up to 4,200 feet (1,300m) in vicinity of cultivated plains. Swarms in orchards and wheat fields. Nests in tree hollows or holes in walls in multiple pairs as community.

DIET Grain mixes for large parrots, fruit, green food.

SPECIAL NEEDS Breeding successful only when couple have aviary to themselves. Aviary at least 6 feet (2m) long, with frost-free protected area.

CAGE LIFE Tolerable voice, gets on with small birds. Before breeding, cover bottom of nest box (8 × 8 × 12 inches/20 × 20 × 30cm, entrance diameter 3 inches/8cm) with wood chips and sawdust. Male begins to court in late winter, sings and runs back and forth in front of female. Lays 2 to 6 eggs, incubation 21 to 23 days by the female, fledging 49 days. Male feeds hen during breeding cycle.

STATUS IN WILD Appendix 2.

Alexandrine Parakeet

Psittacula eupatria
ORDER Psittaciformes FAMILY Psittacidae

DESCRIPTION 18 to 20 inches (45 to 50cm). Prominent black collar around neck with additional pink layer at back. Body mostly green, darker on wings with a reddish shoulder patch. Inner tail feathers are yellowish. Eyes are grey with red circles. Female lacks the black neck collar.

NATURAL DISTRIBUTION Southeast Asia and nearby islands.

HABITAT Forested and cultivated lands; also parks. Usually in small groups that form larger groupings for the night. Nests in holes gnawed in trees, chimneys and naturally occurring hollows.

DIET Seeds, fruit.

SPECIAL NEEDS Large, metal aviary.

CAGE LIFE Can be quite tame, when raised under cage conditions. Fair talker, but must be confined to cage to be taught. Breeding takes place only with ample space. Nest box should be 18 × 16 × 24 inches (45 × 40 × 60cm), with 5 inch (12cm) entrance diameter. Lays 2 to 4 eggs, incubation time 28 days, fledging 40 to 50 days.

STATUS IN WILD Not listed as endangered.

Alexandrine parakeet

Canary-winged parakeet

Canary-Winged Parakeet

Brotogeris versicolorus chiriri
ORDER Psittaciformes FAMILY Psittacidae

DESCRIPTION 8½ to 10 inches (21 to 25cm), tail is 4¼ inches (10.8cm). Primarily green, darker on breast and underneath. Outer wing edges, epaulet and primaries bright yellow. Blue under tail and possibly on wings. Eyes brown, beak pale, legs pinkish. No visible sex distinction, immatures duller.

NATURAL DISTRIBUTION Amazon drainage basin and south over east, central and south Brazil, into north and east Bolivia, Paraguay, north Argentina and eastern Peru.

HABITAT Near forests and towns, in flocks, up to about 50. Nests in tree hollows, nests of tree termites.

DIET Parrot mix, cereal seeds, fruit (especially bananas, which they chew and scatter, producing sticky cage) and green food.

SPECIAL NEEDS Keep only in pairs until brooding time, protect from frost, supply bathing and climbing facilities.

CAGE LIFE Friendly, very tame and good breeder, but may be jealous of other pets. Can mimic sounds and human voice, has a screeching call and may learn a few words. When threatened, raises its wings and claps them together to make explosive sound.

Needs beechwood nest box (8 × 8 × 16 inches/ 20 × 20 × 40cm; entrance diameter 3 inches/8cm) with 1½-inch (4-cm) thick layer of moist peat moss. Lays 3 to 6 white eggs, incubation 23 to 26 days, fledging 50 to 60 days. Male stays on nest at night. Young develop slowly, like to sleep on nest after fledging.

STATUS IN WILD Appendix 2.

Barred Parakeet

LINEOLATED PARAKEET, CATHERINE PARAKEET

Bolborhynchus lineola
ORDER Psittaciformes FAMILY Psittacidae

DESCRIPTION 6½ inches (17cm). Green with yellowish underneath and black shell markings on head, neck, back, rump and along wings. Hen smaller with same, duller markings. Eyes yellow-brown, beak grey-yellow, legs grey-black.

NATURAL DISTRIBUTION Mexico, Panama, Peru and Colombia.

HABITAT Well camouflaged in deep mountain forests in hollow trees, usually in groups, sometimes in flocks of more than 100 after breeding.

DIET Oats, millet spray, sunflower seed kernels, panicum, canary seeds, fresh twigs (apple, pear and willow), berries, carrots, buds, green foods, fruit and small insects. (Rake the aviary a few times a week.)

SPECIAL NEEDS Sensitive to frost. Needs shaded spots and strong branches to slide along. Fast-growing claws need shortening.

CAGE LIFE Gentle, tame and tolerant, with pleasant voice. Excellent runners, they press close to the ground for protection and fan their tails to express emotion. Nesting boxes used all year for roosting. Lays 3 to 6 white eggs in nest box (6 × 6 × 12 inches/15 × 15 × 30cm; entrance diameter 3 inches/8cm. Incubation 19 to 23 days, only by female, fledging 38 to 40 days. Male feeds hen and later young. Good breeding success in colonies.

STATUS IN WILD Appendix 2.

Barred parakeet

Bourke's Parakeet

Neophema boukii
ORDER Psittaciformes FAMILY Psittacidae

DESCRIPTION 8 to 8½ inches (20 to 21 cm). Pink and grey-brown mottling across sides of face through underside of body. Blue above beak, at shoulder patch and on rump, much more pronounced on male. Triangular grey-white eye patch. Brown eyes.

NATURAL DISTRIBUTION Central Australia.

HABITAT Prairie-type areas that feature acacia bushes. The species is somewhat nocturnal. Lives in small flocks. Nests in tree hollows.

DIET Seeds, fruit, insects.

SPECIAL NEEDS Must have a warm, dry environment. Young birds are very wild and can injure themselves against unprotected sides of cage.

CAGE LIFE Nests in tree hollows, or nest box 18 × 6 × 6 inches (45 × 15 × 15cm). Lays 4 to 5 eggs, incubation 18 days by female (fed by male throughout the period), feeding of young by both parents, fledging 28 days.

STATUS IN WILD Not listed as endangered.

Bourke's parakeet

Crimson-Winged Parakeet

Aprosmictus erythropterus erythropterus
ORDER Psittaciformes   FAMILY Psittacidae

DESCRIPTION 13 inches (33cm). Male is bright green – lime on head and underside, forest on back, shoulders and tail – with bright red wing coverts. Female has duller coloration throughout and only a small, indistinct patch of red on the wings. Eyes black encircled with red.

NATURAL DISTRIBUTION Northeast Australia and New Guinea.

HABITAT Open forest areas.

DIET Seeds, greens.

SPECIAL NEEDS Adults are not good community birds. Male tends to harass female during breeding season, unless male primaries are clipped.

CAGE LIFE Nests in tree hollows (particularly eucalyptus) that are up to 30 feet (9m) deep. Lays 3 to 6 eggs, incubation time 21 days, feeding by both parents, fledging 40 days.

STATUS IN WILD Not listed as endangered.

Eastern Rosella

RED ROSELLA, GOLDEN-MANTLED ROSELLA
Platycercus eximius
ORDER Psittaciformes FAMILY Psittacidae

DESCRIPTION 12½ inches (32cm). Bright red head, neck, shoulders and breast; not as brilliant in female. White cheek marks, in female dirty white. Yellow belly, greenish-yellow rump, green back edged in greenish-black. Tail green in centre, then blue, edged in white. Also white cheek and tail marks. Red feathers under the tail. Eyes brown, beak grey, legs dark brown. Immatures achieve adult colouring 10 to 15 months after fledging.

NATURAL DISTRIBUTION Southeastern Australia and Tasmania; introduced to New Zealand.

HABITAT Open grassy terrain spotted with trees and bushes, often near rivers. In large groups or pairs, follows civilization. Partial to ground, can damage cornfields and orchards.

DIET Grass and weed seeds, wheat kernels, grain for large parrots, apples, carrots, green food.

SPECIAL NEEDS Keep in pairs. Aviary at least 13 feet (4m) long. Provide bathing facilities. Tolerates frost.

CAGE LIFE Loud voice, aggressive towards other birds. Excellent breeders and foster parents. Nests in tree hollows and rabbit burrows. Larvae of a moth species live in the nests and eat the faeces of the young. Lays 4 to 8 white eggs, incubation 20 to 22 days by female, male feeds young, fledging 33 to 35 days. Once independent, young should be separated from parents. Breeding possible after pair a year old.

STATUS IN WILD Not listed as endangered.

Eastern rosella

Mealy Rosella

Platycercus adscitus adscitus
ORDER Psittaciformes   FAMILY Psittacidae

DESCRIPTION 9½ inches (22cm). Blue primaries, red shoulder patch, black crown and nape of neck, blue forehead, green underside, brown throat, grey cheek patch.

NATURAL DISTRIBUTION South America.

HABITAT Forests near coastal and river regions. Usually in pairs. Nests in tree hollows.

DIET Seeds, fruit; needs calcium source such as eggshells.

SPECIAL NEEDS Satisfactory community birds with other species, except those of the same genus. Thrives in large, outdoor aviary.

CAGE LIFE Initially shy, but warms quickly to its owners. Nest box should be 9 × 13 inches (22.5 × 32.5cm) with entrance hole diameter of 3 inches (8cm); can be replaced with a hollow log. Lays 3 or 4 eggs. Incubation 26 to 28 days by female. Fledging 42 to 56 days.

STATUS IN WILD Not listed as endangered.

Mealy rosella

Cockatiel

Cockatiel

Nymphicus hollandicus
ORDER Psittaciformes   FAMILY Psittacidae

DESCRIPTION 12 to 14 inches (30 to 35cm). Resembles cockatoo, but has long tail. Although available in other colourings, most common has yellow throat and head with greyish-blue crest and beak, orangish marks on ears, white wing coverts, brown eyes. Known for its variable pied form, borders of white along mostly grey body. Female's facial markings duller and wing coverts greyer. Young resemble female, but the cere is pink, not grey, and tail is shorter.

NATURAL DISTRIBUTION Most of Australia, rarer along coast; introduced to Tasmania.

HABITAT Savannah, grassland, cleared country, near water. Usually in pairs, sometimes in flocks damaging to crops, especially sunflower, sorghum and millet. Nests in tree hollows and close to water. Usually breeds after rainfall.

DIET Grain mixes for medium parrots, plain canary seeds, millet, sunflower seed kernels, hemp, safflower, apples, carrots and green food.

SPECIAL NEEDS Pair by placing inexperienced bird with one that has raised family. Keep tame animals in a room cage, with daily free flight. Will readily breed in roomy aviary when housed by themselves.

CAGE LIFE Graceful and peaceable aviary or cage bird. Can talk and mimic, and cock especially has pleasant song; sometimes noisy. Hisses and swings body when disturbed while nesting. Lives 10 to 25 years. Aviary at least 6½ feet (2m) long. Nest box 13 × 8 × 18 inches (35 × 20 × 45cm), entrance diameter 2⅜ inches (6cm) – low enough so chicks can stick heads out and make peeping/hissing sound and so bird on the nest can see out. Line bottom with sawdust or peat moss. Lays 4 to 8 white eggs, incubation 18 to 21 days (male during day, female at night), fledging 30 to 35 days, fed by parents for some time.

STATUS IN WILD Not listed as endangered.

Lesser Sulphur-Crested Cockatoo

Cacatua sulphurea
ORDER Psittaciformes FAMILY Psittacidae

DESCRIPTION 12 to 14 inches (30 to 36cm). White overall, accented by black beak and legs, yellow to orange crest and wing undersides, paler ear coverts. Eyes black in males, red-brown in females. Iris in immatures changes gradually after second year from grey.

NATURAL DISTRIBUTION Indonesia, Sulawesi (formerly Celebes), Lombok, Sumba, Sumbawa, Flores and Timor; in 6 subspecies.

HABITAT Forests and farmland around civilization and near coast, sometimes in large flocks. Brooding depends on rainy season. Nests in tree hollows.

DIET Parrot mixture, sunflower seeds, corn, wheat millet, pine nuts, berries, fruit, green food.

SPECIAL NEEDS Metal aviary with frost-free sheltered area. Only tame birds suitable for indoors (large cage, supervised freedom on stand). Bathe in rain or under shower.

CAGE LIFE Lively, excitable, friendly, intelligent. Ready to learn tricks. Breeds regularly. Mount nest boxes in dark cage or aviary corners. Lays 2 to 4 white eggs, incubation 27 to 28 days, female at night, male during day, fledging 60 to 65 days, will be fed after that by both parents. As soon as partners begin courting again (bowing head, male circles female), remove the young so they are not attacked by the pair. Psittacine beak and feather disease (PBFD) in young adults is especially prevalent in this species.

STATUS IN WILD Not listed as endangered.

Lesser sulphur-crested cockatoo

Leadbeater's Cockatoo

MAJOR MITCHELL'S COCKATOO

Cacatua leadbeateri
ORDER Psittaciformes FAMILY Psittacidae

DESCRIPTION 13½ to 15¼ inches (34 to 39cm). Prominent feature large, broad crest with red, white and yellow stripes. Body mostly white, with a pinkish tint on underside and head, red brow, white beak, grey legs. Eyes dark brown in male, reddish-brown in female after 3 years.

NATURAL DISTRIBUTION Interior and south-west Australia, in two subspecies.

HABITAT In thick brush of eucalyptis subspecies and in arid country, maybe close to water. In pairs and flocks, usually as families. Nests in tree trunks (especially red gum).

DIET Seeds, fruit.

SPECIAL NEEDS Large aviary.

CAGE LIFE Birds bred in captivity very tame. Fair talker. Nest of decaying trunk with opening about 34 inches (86cm) deep, diameter 10 inches (25cm). Lays 2 to 6 white eggs, incubation time 25 to 30 days by both parents, feeding by both, fledging 28 days.

STATUS IN WILD Not listed as endangered.

Leadbeater's cockatoo

Umbrella Cockatoo

GREAT WHITE COCKATOO,
WHITE-CRESTED COCKATOO
Cacatua alba
ORDER Psittaciformes FAMILY Psittacidae

DESCRIPTION 15¾ to 18 inches (40 to 46cm).
White body, with black eyes (reddish-brown in
female), beak and legs.

NATURAL DISTRIBUTION Northern, south and
central Moluccas.

HABITAT Forest and near farms, in pairs or small
groups.

DIET Seeds, fruit.

SPECIAL NEEDS Large aviary.

CAGE LIFE Friendly, quiet, beautiful, gentle,
easy to tame. Can be long lived, not a good talker.
Aviary breeding rare but possible. Nest box (or
barrel) 19½ × 16½ × 19½ inches (50 × 40 ×
50cm), entrance diameter 5 inches (12cm). Lays
1 to 3 white eggs, incubation 25 to 27 days by
both parents, fledging 11 to 16 weeks, fed by
male for some time after.

STATUS IN WILD Not listed as endangered.

Umbrella cockatoo

Moluccan Cockatoo

SALMON-CRESTED COCKATOO
ROSE-CRESTED COCKATOO

Cacatua moluccensis
ORDER Psittaciformes FAMILY Psittacidae

DESCRIPTION 20 inches (50cm). Feathers larger and broader than most similar-sized birds, resulting in ruffled appearance. Variable body coloration from virtually white to salmon or deep pink, with definite pink on broad, curved crest. Undertail coverts marked yellow, tail itself is short. Eyes blackish (brownish-burgundy in female, grey in immatures), legs and destructive beak dark grey.

NATURAL DISTRIBUTION Southern Moluccas, Ceram, Sapurua, Haruko; introduced to Amboina.

HABITAT Along coast, in forests and on slopes below 3,281 feet (1,000m), in small flocks. Can be destructive on coconut plantations. Nests in high tree hollows.

DIET Fruit, coconuts, berries, insects, sunflower seeds, wheat, corn, oats, peanuts, pine nuts, fruit, parrot mixture and greenstuff.

SPECIAL NEEDS Large aviary for breeding.

CAGE LIFE Good imitator. Gentle and affectionate, but screams and raises its crest when upset. Aviary cage of strong wire mesh with a heated area, stand and branches and roots for gnawing. Nest boxes 47 inches (120cm) high, 31½ inches (80cm) diameter. Lays 1 to 3 white eggs, incubation by both parents 28 to 35 days, fledging 14 to 15 or more weeks.

STATUS IN WILD Not listed as endangered.

Moluccan cockatoo

Peach-faced lovebird

Peach-Faced Lovebird

Agapornis roseicollis
ORDER Psittaciformes FAMILY Psittacidae

DESCRIPTION 6 to 7 inches (15 to 18cm). Mostly bright, accented by pinkish on forehead, cheeks, chin, throat and below; blue on rump and upper-tail coverts. Tail green with black and rust. Yellow or greenish beak, brown eyes, green-grey legs. Female duller and larger than males, immatures greyish-green, and without red accents. Popular mutations are pied, dark factor, yellow, lutino and pastel blue.

NATURAL DISTRIBUTION Southwest Africa.

HABITAT Near water in savannahs up to 5,200 feet (1,585m). Nests in small groups or flocks up to 200 in holes, under roofs, in empty nests. Climbs through vegetation using bills for support.

DIET Cereal seeds, sunflower and safflower seeds, greenstuff, fruit and millet spray.

SPECIAL NEEDS Dry room air creates hatching problems. House independent young in separate pen or aviary.

CAGE LIFE Small, easy to tame, noisy, aggressive towards other species. Pairs, who preen each other, in strong cages 27½ inches (70cm) long, garden aviaries with covered areas, sleeping boxes and willow branches for nesting. Up to three clutches per season. Transports feathers and bark for nest-building materials with rump feathers rather than beak. Lays 4 to 5 white eggs (after second egg, female begins incubation for 22 to 23 days), fledging 30 to 40 days, still fed by male for some time.

STATUS IN WILD Not listed as endangered.

Fischer's Lovebird

Agapornis personata fischeri
ORDER Psittaciformes FAMILY Psittacidae

DESCRIPTION 4 to 6 inches (10 to 15cm). Body shades of green, olive and brown head with orange on forehead and cheeks, golden neck and breast, rump blue, tail green with blue tips. Brown eyes, red beak. Immatures duller with brown markings on upper mandible. No distinction between sexes.

NATURAL DISTRIBUTION Africa, south and south-east of Lake Victoria.

HABITAT Savannahs at elevations 3,281–22,966 feet (1,000–7,000m). Small flocks, nests in tree hollows. Flocks to fields at wheat-ripening time.

DIET Cereal seeds, sunflower and safflower seeds, grain mixes, greenfood and fruit.

SPECIAL NEEDS Pairs. Fresh branches, bathing dishes. Sensitive to frost.

CAGE LIFE Attractive, easy to accommodate, sociable in aviary, possibly nervous. Flies straight and fast, making rustling noise with wings. Cage at least 27½ inches (70cm) long with strong mesh. Nest boxes used year round for roosting. Lays 4 to 6 white eggs, incubation 20 to 25 days, fledging 35 to 40 days, totally independent 10 to 12 days after that.

STATUS IN WILD Not listed as endangered.

Fischer's lovebird

Masked Lovebird

WHITE EYE-RING LOVEBIRD,
YELLOW-COLLARED LOVEBIRD

Agapornis personata personata
ORDER Psittaciformes FAMILY Psittacidae

DESCRIPTION 5½ to 6 inches (14 to 15.5cm). Dark brown head, yellow collar and breast, yellow-orange throat and chest yellow, body green, blue rump and tail, which has black and red band near ends on outer feathers. Brown eyes, red bill, grey legs. Immatures duller with black on beak. Females weigh more than males. Blue mutation also available.

NATURAL DISTRIBUTION Northern Tanzania; introduced into Kenya.

HABITAT Nomadic. Grassy prairies with some trees. Nests in abandoned nests, breeds in 2¾ inch (7cm) space between tiles of roof and boarding underneath. Broods in colonies. Visits corn and millet fields.

DIET Cereal seeds, sunflower and safflower seeds, grain mixes, green food and fruit.

SPECIAL NEEDS Pairs. Cage with sleeping box and shallow bathing dishes. Free, supervised flight in house. Susceptible to frost, gnaws fresh branches for building.

CAGE LIFE Attractive and quiet. Distinctive coloration. Male scratches its head with feet before mating, female lines nests. Provide more boxes than pairs, 19¾ × 10 inches (50 × 25cm). Lays 3 to 6 eggs, incubation 21 to 23 days, fledging 40 to 46 days.

STATUS IN WILD Not listed as endangered.

Masked lovebird (top left and bottom centre)

Peach-Fronted Conure

GOLDEN-CROWNED CONURE

Aratinga aurea
ORDER Psittaciformes FAMILY Psittacidae

DESCRIPTION 11 inches (28cm). Yellowish-orange head bordered with blue, with orange eye ring. Dark green rump and neck, body mostly pale with yellow-green front, blue tint on wing feathers. Orange-brown eyes, legs dark grey. Immatures like parents.

NATURAL DISTRIBUTION Brazil, Bolivia, Paraguay and northwestern Argentina.

HABITAT Savannah woods and open country, in pairs or flocks (up to 30 birds). Habitat widening because of land clearing. Nests in tree hollows.

DIET Searches for food in trees and on ground. Grass seeds, hemp, oats, grain mix for large parrots, fruits, fresh buds, boiled or soaked seeds, corn, soaked white bread, live food (mealworms, white worms, 'ant-eggs'), nuts, berries, apples, hard-boiled eggs, insects.

SPECIAL NEEDS Bathing facilities and roosting boxes.

CAGE LIFE Abundant, easy to breed, tame, loud voice, can be taught a few words, becomes attached to keeper, tolerates other species only outside brooding period; defends nest even against caretaker. Lives more than 20 years. Aviary at least 6½ feet (2m) long, a little gnawing on wooden construction. Nest box 14 × 10 × 10 inches (35 × 25 × 25cm), entrance 3 inches (8cm). Lays 2 to 6 white eggs, incubation 26 days by both partners, care by male only after 28 days, fledging 50 days. After young leave, remove all fellow species from aviary because male will actively defend young. Two broods per season possible.

STATUS IN WILD Not listed as endangered.

Peach-fronted conure

Sun Conure

Aratinga solstitialis
ORDER Psittaciformes FAMILY Psittacidae

DESCRIPTION 12 inches (30cm). Orange head and belly, breast yellow, small primaries yellow edged in green, large primaries blue. White eye ring, smaller on female. Eyes brown, beak charcoal, legs grey. Immatures less colourful, more green, less orange, black eye. Female more green on wings.

NATURAL DISTRIBUTION Northeastern South America.

HABITAT Forests, savannahs and palm groves, in flocks. Nests in palm tree cavities. Gathers to feed in treetops.

DIET Parrot mixture, smaller cereal seeds, fruit, greenstuff, blossoms and nuts.

SPECIAL NEEDS Recently imported birds cannot be kept at temperature below 68°F (20°C).

CAGE LIFE Gives shrill, two-note screeches; an expressive bird. During the breeding season, males become excited when keeper enters the aviary and checks the nest box. Sleeps in tree hole or nest box, 16 × 10 × 10 inches (40 × 25 × 25cm), entrance diameter 3 inches (8cm) or 12-inch (30cm) cube. Lays 3 to 6 eggs, incubation 27 days by female, fledging 56 days but young still fed by both parents and spend night in original nesting box. More susceptible to vice of feather plucking than related species, and adults may even pluck immatures.

STATUS IN WILD Not listed as endangered.

Sun conure

Cactus conure

Cactus Conure

Aratinga actorum
ORDER Psittaciformes FAMILY Psittacidae

DESCRIPTION 10 to 11 inches (25 to 26cm). Brownish-green on head, gradually turning olive down back and on wings, lighter brown under chin, turning to orange rust below breast.

NATURAL DISTRIBUTION Brazil.

HABITAT South American rainforest.

DIET In the wild, primarily cactus seeds (hence its name), and fruit and berries.

SPECIAL NEEDS Stays relatively peaceful with other conures.

CAGE LIFE Makes up for lack of bright colour with friendly, even affectionate, personality. Suitable for roomy cage or aviary. Lays 3 to 4 white eggs, incubation 28 to 30 days, fledging 40 days.

STATUS IN WILD Not listed as endangered.

Blue-Crowned Conure

Aratinga acuticaudata
ORDER Psittaciformes FAMILY Psittacidae

DESCRIPTION 14½ inches (37cm). Body green with yellow showing underneath. Forehead and part of head showing blue. White ring on light brown eyes. Beak pale, legs brownish. Immatures sometimes have red spots on shoulders or wing edges.

NATURAL DISTRIBUTION Northern Venezuela, Brazil and Colombia.

HABITAT Forest near farmland and fruit trees, sometimes large flocks.

DIET Seeds, fruit, berries.

SPECIAL NEEDS Fruits and berries essential in diet.

CAGE LIFE Intelligent and affectionate, with possibly overpowering voice. May learn to talk. Long nest box or hollow tree. Lays 3 eggs, incubation 24 days, fledging 56 days, fed by male.

STATUS IN WILD Not listed as endangered.

White-Eared Conure

Pyrrhura leucotis
ORDER Psittaciformes FAMILY Psittacidae

DESCRIPTION 9 inches (23cm). Brown head, beak area and sides of face, with whitish ear coverts. Neck and throat bright blue, turning green on breast, with black and white half-circle shapes down to reddish-brown belly. Tail brownish, wings bluer and green. Eyes orangish-brown, beak and legs black. Female has bolder head and beak.

NATURAL DISTRIBUTION Coastal portions of Venezuela and Brazil; introduced into Rio de Janeiro.

HABITAT High tropical and subtropical trees, in small group up to 25.

DIET Insects, larvae, termites, fruits, seeds.

SPECIAL NEEDS Immatures need supplements of soaked stale white bread, cooked corn, sunflower seeds, boiled potatoes, hemp, oats, carrot strips, fresh twigs and leaf buds.

CAGE LIFE One of the most popular smaller conures, pleasant and easy to tame. Closed nest box, preferably of beech, 10 × 10 × 14 inches (25 × 25 × 35cm), entrance 3 inches (8cm). Lays 5 to 9 eggs, incubation 22 days by female days and male nights, male feeds partner during day, fledging 35 to 38 days.

STATUS IN WILD Not listed as endangered.

White-eared conure

Red-Bellied Conure

MAROON-BELLIED CONURE

Pyrrhura frontalis
ORDER Psittaciformes FAMILY Psittacidae

DESCRIPTION 9 to 10 inches (23 to 26cm). Body green, chin and breast grey-green, darker at ends. Brownish band on forehead and patches on ears, lower back and centre underneath. Wing coverts bluish. Tail copper at base and end. Beak blackish, eyes orangish-red, legs dark grey. White eye ring. No visible sex distinction. Immatures duller with shorter tails.

NATURAL DISTRIBUTION South America: Brazil to Uruguay, Paraguay and Argentina.

HABITAT Forests, farmland, orchards, corn fields, sometimes in large flocks seeking bloom-ing trees and fields with ripening wheat. Breeds in tree hollows.

DIET Parrot mix, small pine nuts, cereal seeds, greenstuff, millet, fresh corncobs, fruit, insects and larvae.

SPECIAL NEEDS Breeding results best if pair housed on its own in quiet, protected aviary. Can be restless, best to attach natural branches to mesh of aviary to avoid injury.

CAGE LIFE Relatively quiet compared to other conures. Easy to tame, lively and inquisitive. Nest box 10 × 10 × 14 inches (25 × 25 × 35cm), entrance 3 inches (8cm). Lays 4 to 6 eggs, in-cubation 24 to 28 days only by female, fledging 45 to 50 days, taken care of by male.

STATUS IN WILD Not listed as endangered.

Red-bellied conure

Nandaya Conure

BLACK-HEADED CONURE,
BLACK-MASKED CONURE

Nandayus nenday
ORDER Psittaciformes · FAMILY Psittacidae

DESCRIPTION 12 inches (30cm). Green with blackish cap, upper throat, and below eyes. Blue on throat and upper breast, bluish-black wings. Olive tail with bluish-black point, underneath dark green to black. Thighs red set off by black legs. Eyes reddish-brown, beak charcoal.

NATURAL DISTRIBUTION North Argentina, Paraguay, south-east Bolivia, southern Mato Grosso.

HABITAT Savannahs, woods, palm country, rice fields. May be in large flocks. Nests in tree hollows.

DIET Grain, seeds, fruit.

SPECIAL NEEDS Much too loud to keep indoors. Hang nest box low enough so it can watch its world and make commentary.

CAGE LIFE Can be kept together with finches. Likes to bathe or hop in rain shower. Tamable, easy breeder, good talker of limited vocabulary, but has a raucous call. Will take treats out of keeper's hand. Nest box 12 × 12 × 14 inches (30 × 30 × 40cm), entrance diameter 3 inches (8cm). Lays 2 to 5 white eggs, incubation 25 days (when female is incubating, male sits silently on top of box), fledging 50 to 55 days.

STATUS IN WILD Not listed as endangered.

Nandaya conure

Blue-Winged Conure

PAINTED CONURE

Pyrrhura picta
ORDER Psittaciformes FAMILY Psittacidae

DESCRIPTION 18 to 20 inches (45 to 50cm). Prominent black collar around neck with additional pink layer at back. Body mostly green, darker on wings with a reddish shoulder patch. Inner tail feathers are yellowish. Eyes are grey with red circles. Female lacks the black neck collar.

NATURAL DISTRIBUTION Southeast Asia and nearby islands.

HABITAT Forested and cultivated lands; also parks. Usually in small groups that form larger groupings for the night. Nests in holes gnawed in trees, chimneys and naturally occurring hollows.

DIET Seeds, fruit.

SPECIAL NEEDS Large, metal aviary.

CAGE LIFE Can be quite tame, when raised under cage conditions. Fair talker, but must be confined to cage to be taught. Breeding takes place only with ample space. Nestbox should be 18 × 16 × 24 inches (45 × 40 × 60cm), with 5 inch (12cm) entrance diameter. Lays 2–4 eggs, incubation time 28 days, fledging 40 to 50 days.

STATUS IN WILD Not listed as endangered.

Blue-winged conure

Monk Parakeet

**QUAKER PARAKEET,
GREY-BREASTED PARAKEET**

Myiopsitta monachus
ORDER Psittaciformes FAMILY Psittacidae

DESCRIPTION 12 inches (30cm). Body green. Forehead, face, neck and breast greyish-blue. Cheeks pale grey. Back of head, neck, back, rump, wings and tail parrot-green. Eyes and beak brown, legs grey. Blue and yellow mutations.

NATURAL DISTRIBUTION Southern Brazil to central Argentina; introduced to New York, New Jersey and Connecticut. Nests recorded in Massachusetts, Virginia and Florida.

HABITAT Lowland, woods, farmland, savannahs, woods, orchards. Follows civilization, damages fields.

DIET Mixed grain for large parrots, fruit, carrots, green food.

SPECIAL NEEDS Unlikely to breed unless housing has generous dimensions and shrubbery is plentiful.

CAGE LIFE Peaceful and pleasant, has exaggerated reputation as screamer. Close pair bonding. Can be maintained flying free; damages garden. Only parrot species to build proper nest. Bullet-shaped nest or nest boxes 6 × 12 × 17½ inches (15 × 30 × 45cm), entrance 3 inches (8cm) with two 'rooms', entrance protected by a small portico. Lays 5 to 8 eggs, incubated in 'back room' 26 to 28 days, fledging 42 to 44 days. After brooding period, symbolic feeding of partner serves as a sign of belonging together.

STATUS IN WILD Appendix 2.

Monk parakeet

Celestial Parrotlet

PACIFIC PARROTLET
Forpus coelestis
ORDER Psittaciformes FAMILY Psittacidae

DESCRIPTION 4¾ inches (12cm). Green, plus blue in wings, on rump and on narrow band along back of neck. Eyes brown, beak greyish, legs pinkish. Female less clearly defined, lacks blue in wings.

NATURAL DISTRIBUTION Tropical areas of western South America.

HABITAT Woody areas, but not thick rain forests, in colonies. Breeds in hollow trees, branches or ground holes.

DIET Fruit.

SPECIAL NEEDS Newly imported birds must be kept at room temperature. Pairs must be alone to breed.

CAGE LIFE Ideal cage bird. Can be kept with several pairs together if no breeding expected. Breeding pairs attack each other's legs, especially during breeding season. Give pair normal budgerigar nest box with peat moss or wood shavings on the bottom. Lays 4 to 6 eggs, incubation 17 to 21 days by female, fledging 30 to 34 days. May breed two or three times a year, beginning in April.

STATUS IN WILD Not listed as endangered.

Celestial parrotlet

Green-Rumped Parrotlet

Forpus passerinus
ORDER Psittaciformes   FAMILY Psittacidae

DESCRIPTION 4¾ inches (12cm). All green, brighter on face, forehead and rump, lighter underneath. Turquoise tint on wing, pale beak.

NATURAL DISTRIBUTION Venezuela, Trinidad and Colombia.

HABITAT Wooded areas.

DIET Sunflower and safflower seeds, canary seeds, cereal, nuts, fruits, garden vegetables, green foods, dates, figs.

SPECIAL NEEDS Varied diet.

CAGE LIFE Nest box 5 × 5 × 8 inches (13 × 13 × 20cm), entrance 1½ inches (4cm). Lays 4 to 7 white eggs, deposited on alternate days, incubation 21 to 23 days by female only, male feeds her and later young, fledging 30 to 35 days. Young fed by both parents at least another 14 days. Separate fledgings from parents once they become independent, allowing female to start on next brood. Up to three broods per year.

STATUS IN WILD Not listed as endangered.

Green-rumped parrotlet

Red Lory

MOLUCCAN LORY

Eos bornea

ORDER Psittaciformes FAMILY Psittacidae

DESCRIPTION 10 to 12¼ inches (25 to 31cm). Red with blue vent and undertail coverts. Black and red wings, blue coverts. Eyes red, beak orange, legs charcoal. Tongue has elongated papillae on tip that become erect when feeding.

NATURAL DISTRIBUTION Indonesia: Ambon, Saparua, Foram, Ceramlaut, Watubela and Kai Islands; and the Moluccas.

HABITAT Coastal and mountain forest up to 4,000 feet (1,250m), in flowering trees, in group and sometimes in large flocks. Nests in cavities high in mature trees.

DIET Nectar, pollen and fruit supplemented with seeds and grain. Look for commercial lory foods. Offer on feeder 5 feet (1.5m) from the ground.

SPECIAL NEEDS Sudden change in diet could lead to changes in bacterial population within gut, which could precipitate fatal bout of enterotoxaemia. During winter, house inside, at about 75°F (24°C).

CAGE LIFE Gentle, playful with harsh voice. Best in pairs. Once acclimatized, can be kept in outdoor aviary. Roosts in nest box 14 × 14 × 18 inches (35 × 35 × 45cm), entrance diameter 3½ inches (9cm). Lays 2 eggs, incubation 23 to 25 days by female, male sleeps next to her at night, fledging 90 days, fed by both parents another 2 to 3 weeks.

STATUS IN WILD Appendix 2.

Red lory

Chattering lory

Chattering Lory

Lorius garrulus
ORDER Psittaciformes FAMILY Psittacidae

DESCRIPTION 12 inches (30cm). Glowing, deep red overall. Wings and thighs brown-green. Front edge of wing and underwing coverts yellow, primaries grey underneath with reddish band. Uppertail brown-green with blue tips. Eyes yellowish-brown to red, beak orange, legs charcoal. Immatures have brown beaks and dark brown irises. No visible means of distinguishing sexes.

NATURAL DISTRIBUTION Moluccan islands of Indonesia.

HABITAT Forest regions, around flowering coconut and palm trees in pairs (in their own territories) or flocks. Broods in tree hollows.

DIET Nectar and fruit, with greenstuff and some seed. Supplement with vitamin A to avoid fungal disease candidiasis. Also provide pollen, a natural for this group.

SPECIAL NEEDS Bathing facilities (even though they may splash water around the room). Keep in pairs, temperature not below 50°F (10°C).

CAGE LIFE Loud voice, imitator, messy eater, tame. May learn to talk. Aggressive towards other pairs of same species and towards caretaker. Breeding necessary for preservation of stock. Better suited for aviary than cage. Lays 2 eggs, incubation 24 to 28 days, male sleeps in nest at night, fledging 75 days, male can then be hostile to young.

STATUS IN WILD Appendix 2.

Blue-and-Yellow Macaw

BLUE-AND-GOLD MACAW

Ara ararauna

ORDER Psittaciformes FAMILY Psittacidae

DESCRIPTION 34 to 36 inches (86 to 90cm). Back and wings turquoise. Sides of neck, breast and belly golden. Forehead and crown greenish-blue. Throat black, cheeks white bordered in black stripes. Bluish-yellow undertail coverts. Eyes yellow, beak and legs black. Female is smaller, immatures have dark eyes.

NATURAL DISTRIBUTION Panama southwards into Central America to northern Paraguay.

HABITAT Close to water in forests, savannahs, open country and swamps in regions up to 1,500 feet (500m), in pairs or flocks up to 100. Nests in holes of dead palm trees.

DIET Leaves, seeds, fruits, nuts, parrot food, mealworms, cheese, greenstuff.

SPECIAL NEEDS Their strong beaks can find weakness in the design and construction of their housing.

CAGE LIFE Affectionate, loyal, gentle, intelligent. Can learn tricks and to imitate and talk. Can live 100 years or more. May become aggressive towards keepers during breeding season. Roomy cages of mesh with climbing branches, heated covered areas and – as playthings – fresh branches, pinecones and stones. Nest box, year round for roosting, 20 × 20 × 31½ inches (50 × 50 × 80cm), entrance 5½ inches (14cm). Lays 2 to 5 white eggs, incubation 25 to 28 days, fledging after 3 months.

STATUS IN WILD Appendix 2.

Blue-and-yellow macaw

African Grey Parrot

GREY PARROT

Psittacus erithacus
ORDER Psittaciformes FAMILY Psittacidae

DESCRIPTION 13 to 14 inches (33 to 36cm). Body dove-grey with lighter grey unfeathered face, red tail and under coverts, yellow eyes (round in male, oblong in female), black beak, charcoal legs. Female smaller in head, beak and body, and lighter on underside. Immature iris black, changes to grey.

NATURAL DISTRIBUTION Central Africa.

HABITAT Forests, savannah, mangroves, often in large flocks up to 5,000. Chooses tall trees to sleep in at night. Breeds in loose colonies, each pair occupying its own tree. Loves to shower in the rain.

DIET Parrot food, nuts, grains, fruit and green-stuff.

SPECIAL NEEDS Check newly imported for bacterial infections, especially salmonella. Males won't breed until second or third year, females fifth or sixth.

CAGE LIFE A renowned cage bird, affectionate. Probably the best talking parrot, with remarkable talent for mimicry, but not noisy. May be a 'growler'. An agitated bird will oscillate pupils and raise nape feathers. Intelligent and sensitive nature makes it susceptible to vice of feather plucking, which can become a habit. Large cage 25½ × 20 × 31½ inches (65 × 50 × 80cm). Nest box 16 × 18 × 26 inches (40 × 45 × 65cm), entrance 6 inches (15cm). Lays 2 to 4 eggs in cavity, incubation 29 days by female, fed by male on nest, fledging 10 to 11 weeks, fed by both parents for another 4 months.

STATUS IN WILD Appendix 2.

African grey parrot

Blue-Fronted Amazon Parrot

Amazona aestiva
ORDER Psittaciformes FAMILY Psittacidae

DESCRIPTION 13½ to 16 inches (35 to 41cm). Green body with bluish forehead and yellow throat, cheeks and crown. Wing coverts red and wing bend red or yellow. Eyes orange, beak black, legs grey. Immatures duller with black eyes. No visible distinction between sexes.

NATURAL DISTRIBUTION Brazil, Bolivia, Paraguay, northern Argentina, in two subspecies.

HABITAT Tropical woods, bush country. Broods in tree hollows, in large flocks after brooding. Nomadic.

DIET Fruits, berries, greens, fresh corncobs, germinated sunflower seeds, half-ripe wheat, grain mix for parrots.

SPECIAL NEEDS Fruits and berries essential in diet, as is wood for chewing.

CAGE LIFE Excellent talking and mimic ability. Attractive and responsive to training. May be aggressive towards keeper during breeding season. Aviary with climbing branches, heatable covered area. Spray during warm weather. Use a hollow log or nest box 24 × 12 × 12 inches (60 × 30 × 30cm), entrance 6 inches (15cm), with a layer of peat mould. Lays 2 to 5 white eggs, incubation 27 to 29 days, fledging 9 weeks.

STATUS IN WILD Appendix 2.

Blue-fronted Amazon parrot

Electus Parrot

GRAND ELECTUS

Electus roratus
ORDER Psittaciformes   FAMILY Psittacidae

DESCRIPTION 14 to 15 inches (35 to 38cm). Because sexes are so differently coloured, they were once thought to be two species. Male mostly green, female red. Male's upper mandible is coral with yellow tip, lower mandible almost black, iris orange and legs grey. Female's beak black, iris yellowish. Female more dominant than male.

NATURAL DISTRIBUTION Moluccas, Ceram, Sumba, Halmahera, Solomon Islands, New Guinea and islands, and northern Queensland (Australia), in 10 subspecies.

HABITAT Forest and mountain regions up to 3,281 feet (1,000m) elevation. Strong flyers, they breed high in tree holes several feet deep with entrance more than 65½ feet (20m) high.

DIET Sunflower seeds, millet, canary grass seed, peanuts, pine nuts, millet spray, cooked rice, fruit, fresh corn on the cob, green peas, carrots, celery, tomatoes, green food, milk-soaked bread, raisins, berries, flower buds, lettuce, dandelion, spinach and chickweed.

SPECIAL NEEDS Imported birds need warm (71°F/22°C) indoor aviaries (only one pair per aviary), and available fresh water. High vitamin A requirement.

CAGE LIFE At first they refuse all food. Female often more delicate than male, and may stir up trouble in the aviary before settling down with her partner. Roomy cage at least 1 cubic yard or 13 feet (4m) long with heatable covered area. Nest box 12 × 12 × 20 inches (30 × 30 × 50cm), entrance 6 inches (15cm). Lays 2 eggs, incubation 28 day, fledging 10 to 11 weeks.

STATUS IN WILD Appendix 2.

Electus parrot

Yellow-Fronted Amazon Parrot

YELLOW-CROWNED AMAZON

Amazona ochrocephala
ORDER Psittaciformes FAMILY Psittacidae

DESCRIPTION 14 to 15¾ inches (35 to 40cm). Green with golden crown and red wing coverts, bend and edge of wing. Eyes orange, beak grey with orange, legs grey. Immatures have dark irises. No visible means of sex distinction.

NATURAL DISTRIBUTION Mexico, Central America and tropical portions of South America; introduced to California and Florida. Nine subspecies.

HABITAT Forests, woods, cultivated fields, savannahs, in pairs or flocks. Some subspecies follow civilization. Nests in tree holes, termite nests or holes in ground. Gathers in groups in treetops to forage, returning at dusk, flying with characteristic shallow wing beats below body level, like those of ducks. During breeding may copulate several times a day.

DIET Sunflower seed kernels, corn, wheat, oats, peanuts, pine nuts, parrot mix, fruit, berries, blossoms, green food.

SPECIAL NEEDS Large, strong cage. Keep in pairs in outdoor aviary.

CAGE LIFE Tames readily and talks well, but does not mimic despite its reputation as a mimic. Produces metallic shrieks, whistling contacts and squawks. Likes human company. Keep free on parrot stand. Heatable protected space, facilities for bathing (spray). Nest box 18 × 18 × 29½ inches (45 × 45 × 75cm), entrance diameter 5½ inches (14cm). Lays 2 to 3 eggs, incubation 28 to 30 days by female, fledging 75 days.

STATUS IN WILD Appendix 2.

Yellow-fronted Amazon parrot

Mexican red-headed parrot

Mexican Red-Headed Parrot

GREEN-CHEEKED AMAZON PARROT
Amazona viridigenalis
ORDER Psittaciformes FAMILY Psittacidae

DESCRIPTION 13 inches (33cm). Green with black edges on feathers. Red cap covers down to the eyes and nearly to the nape, hint of lavender eyebrow. Blue crown, red wing coverts, yellow tip on tail. Yellow eyes, pale beak, grey legs.

NATURAL DISTRIBUTION Northern Mexico.

HABITAT Forests and in lowlands, near water. Forages in cypress and acacia trees, in pairs or large flocks.

DIET Large sunflower seeds, boiled corn, hemp, oats, wheat, white seed, millet, walnuts, hazelnuts, ground nuts, fruit, greens and berries such as black currants, rowan berries, bilberries, gooseberries and strawberries.

SPECIAL NEEDS Fruits and berries essential in diet, as is wood for chewing.

CAGE LIFE Gentle and popular, good talker. Courtship accompanied by shrieking and pecking at each other. Aviary with roomy barrel or nest box. Lays 2 to 3 eggs, incubation 26 days, fledging 68 days.

STATUS IN WILD Appendix 2.

Scarlet Macaw

Ara macao
ORDER Psittaciformes FAMILY Psittacidae

DESCRIPTION 33½ inches (85cm). Body deep red, shoulders and wings yellow. Primaries and tail coverts blue, greater wing coverts and shoulder coverts yellow, undersides of wings red-brown. Lower back and rump light blue. Cheek region bare and white with red feather lines. Eyes yellow, upper mandible pale with black at base, lower mandible and legs charcoal. Female smaller with shorter, broader beak.

NATURAL DISTRIBUTION Southern Mexico, Central America and northern South America. More widely distributed than any other macaw species.

HABITAT Light woodland and savannah, low-lying humid areas up to 1,300 feet (400m), in pairs, family parties or flocks up to about 25 birds. They can often be observed flying in pairs, their wings nearly touching. Fly up to 18½ miles (30km) to feed on palm fruit, figs, mangoes and beetle larvae. Noisy in flight but feed in silence.

DIET Oranges, bananas, sunflower seeds, nuts, berries, carrots, calcium (cuttlefish bone), bread, tomatoes, fresh twigs, fresh corn on the cob.

SPECIAL NEEDS Fresh branches for occupation.

CAGE LIFE Sociable bird, usually monogamous in pairs, affectionate towards keeper. Can be noisy, especially when frustrated or bored, screeches. Loves to bathe, slaps water onto itself with its wings. Roomy aviary, parrot stands. Large nest box 23½ × 23½ × 25½ inches (60 × 60 × 65cm) all year, also for roosting. Lays 2 to 4 eggs, incubation 26 days, only by female, male sits at her side, fledging 90 days, chicks remain with parents for some time after.

STATUS IN WILD Appendix 1.

Scarlet macaw

Military Macaw

GREAT GREEN MACAW

Ara militaris

ORDER Psittaciformes FAMILY Psittacidae

DESCRIPTION 25½ inches (65cm). Olive with red forehead, blue uppertail coverts and rump, bluish-red primary feathers. Cheek patches with rows of violet-brown feathers. Eyes yellow, beak charcoal, legs light grey. Female smaller. Immatures duller with brownish tint.

NATURAL DISTRIBUTION Mexico to Argentina, in three subspecies.

HABITAT Dry forest and open woodland, in pairs or small flocks up to about 20. Like other macaws, they leave in morning to forage and return to roosting spots at dusk.

DIET Nuts, berries, fruits, greens.

SPECIAL NEEDS Barrels or drums for pairs.

CAGE LIFE Easily tamed, friendly bird, moderate talking ability. Lays 2 to 3 eggs, incubation 28 days, fledging after 3 months.

STATUS IN WILD Appendix 1.

Military macaw

Rainbow Lorikeet

**SWAINSON'S LORIKEET,
BLUE MOUNTAIN LORIKEET**

Trichoglossus haematodus moluccanus
ORDER Psittaciformes   FAMILY Psittacidae

DESCRIPTION 11 to 12 inches (28 to 30cm). Patched in a variety of colours. Violet to blue head and belly. Yellow on back of head and mixed with green shades on back and wings. Breast red with yellow. Undertail coverts and underside of tail yellow and green. Underwing coverts orange. Eyes orange-red, beak orange-red, legs greenish-grey.

NATURAL DISTRIBUTION Northeastern Australia and nearby areas, one of 21 subspecies scattered over the southwest Pacific.

HABITAT Lowlands, savannahs, woodlands, secondary forests, along water, up to 6,500 feet (2,000m), in pairs or small (noisy) flocks of 5 to 20 birds. Avoids ground, prefers to bathe in damp foliage or rain. Broods in tree hollows. Spends the night in great communal roosts, maybe of thousands.

DIET Fruits, insects, pollen, nectar (they are important pollinators of coconut flowers), sunflower seeds, oats, ripened grain, canary-grass seeds, spray millet, buckwheat, apples, grapes, carrots, mealworms.

SPECIAL NEEDS Keep in pairs in a long aviary with a roomy night shelter, temperature at 75°F (24°C). Facilities for bathing and perching. Does not get on with other species.

CAGE LIFE Prolific breeder. Digs holes in ground or nest boxes 10 × 10 × 18 inches (25 × 25 × 45cm), entrance 3½ inches (9cm). Lays 2 eggs, incubation 24 to 26 days, fledging 75 to 80 days.

STATUS IN WILD Not listed as endangered.

Rainbow lorikeet

Budgerigar

Melopsittacus undulatus
ORDER Psittaciformes FAMILY Psittacidae

DESCRIPTION 7 inches (18cm). Green with yellow forehead and cheeks. Horizontal black and yellow bands on back. Cere blue in male, brown in female. Many mutations. Immatures may show barring on head down to cere. Beaks of newly fledged may be dark, their eyes solid lacking white irises.

NATURAL DISTRIBUTION Australia, except eastern coastal areas and Tasmania. Nomadic by nature. Brought to Europe in 19th century, now one of most popular of all cage birds.

HABITAT Grassland with a few trees, close to water. In dry spells millions of budgerigars gather in watery areas. Travels in nomadic flocks. Nests in tree hollows, such as eucalyptus knotholes. Brooding period dependent on food supply (rainy season). Collects seeds from ground vegetation including grasses and weeds.

DIET Millet, canary grass seeds, oats, greenstuff, carrots, sweet apples.

SPECIAL NEEDS Indoor birds need iodine.

CAGE LIFE Inexpensive, easy to care for. Most common bird species in captivity. Sociable, quick to tame, and can prove a talented talker. Keep in pairs, or dolls and other toys serve as substitute partners. Large cage with gauge, daily free flight in the room. Nest box from poplar or birch, which should be removed in August to prevent attempts to rear chicks during colder months; replace the following spring. Lays 4 to 8 eggs, up to 10 in as little as 10 days, incubation 18 days, fledging 20 days.

STATUS IN WILD Not listed as endangered.

Budgerigar

Domestic Canary

Serinus canarius domesticus
ORDER Psittaciformes FAMILY Psittacidae

DESCRIPTION 4 to 8 inches (10 to 20cm), depending on the breed. Some have been developed for body type, some for coloration, some for singing ability. The variety of forms and colours bred from the wild greenish-coloured species is considerable because it is impossible to produce birds of all types in three different ground colours: yellow, white and buff. Ground colour of the wild bird is yellow and, like the other two colours, is divided into two feather textures, known as yellow and buff. Feathers of the yellow are shorter, firmer and richer than those of the buff, the feathers of which are longer, softer and appear less deep in shade. Feathers of buff have paler edging, usually more noticeable on the back of neck and head. Whites are more tightly feathered than the buff. Yellow should be paired with buff. If two yellows are mated, feathers become tight and birds are too slim. When two buffs are bred it results in fluffy, over-feathered offspring. Immatures smaller with shorter tails. Cocks distinguished from females by song.

NATURAL DISTRIBUTION Does not occur in the wild. Descended from Wild Canaries (*S.C. canarius*), found on islands off northwestern coast of Africa, including the Canary Islands. Wild canaries introduced to Europe, and may have been crossed with native songsters, such as the Serin (*S. serinus*). Early in the 16th century, yellow and white variants were recorded and selective breeding began in earnest, which has given rise to wide variety of breeds today. Best known of singing category is Roller Canary, which originated in Germany around the Harz Mountain region.

HABITAT Cages and aviaries.

DIET Canary seed mixture, with plain canary seed and red rape, plus other seeds such as niger, and greenstuff.

SPECIAL NEEDS If interested in a singer, obtain a cock no matter what the breed. Housing two birds in separate cages in same room often stimulates competition, encouraging both to sing for long periods. Do not house two cocks together because they are liable to fight.

Canary

CAGE LIFE Can breed in home if in a breeding cage with nesting pan attached inside. Pan should be lined with piece of felt and hen provided with safe nesting material. Lays 4 eggs, 1 each day. Remove the first 3, store in matchbox lined with cotton wool, replace them with dummy eggs. On fourth day, restore first 3 and hen will start to incubate. This ensures they will be of similar age when hatched, more likely to survive. Remove the cock bird just before laying to allow hen to rear chicks on her own. Alternatively, the pair can be left together throughout. Incubation 13 days, fledging another 13. Offer rearing food throughout this period, introduce seed gradually.

STATUS IN WILD Not listed as endangered.

Green Singing Finch

YELLOW-EYED CANARY

Serinus mozambicus
ORDER Passeriformes FAMILY Fringillidae

DESCRIPTION 5 inches (12.5cm). Greenish-grey upperparts, yellow rump and underneath. Yellow eyebrow, throat and chin. Females duller, and young females have necklace of 5 to 7 small black spots across throat. Eyes and legs dark brown, beak pale.

NATURAL DISTRIBUTION Africa, south of the Sahara.

HABITAT Gardens, parks, woodland.

DIET Canary and live food.

SPECIAL NEEDS Will breed more readily in large cage or indoor aviary where a reasonably warm temperature can be maintained.

CAGE LIFE Long-lived, hardy, bright. Can be kept in large, well-planted aviary. Male has hearty song during breeding season and can be aggressive towards small finches and waxbills. Pairs only for breeding season, and afterward separates. Mating behaviour, lasting about a week, is rough and can result in loss of many of female's feathers. They build open-type nest box or free cup-shaped nest. Lays 3 to 4 pale-blue eggs, incubation 13 to 14 days, only by female, fledging 18 days. Male feeds female on nest.

STATUS IN WILD Not listed as endangered.

Green singing finch

Zebra Finch

Taeniopygia (poephila) guttata
ORDER Passeriformes FAMILY Estrildidae

DESCRIPTION 4 inches (10cm). Greyish-blue on head and neck, turning to duller greyish-brown back and wings, and black tail with white diagonal bands. Bluish-grey chest with black wavy markings, lower chest black, belly almost white. Sides orangish-red with white round marks, white 'moustache', black band under eye marks front edge of orange ear spots. Eyes and beak red, legs brownish. Female grey on top with almost-white ear mark, and grey on throat, neck, chest and sides. Immatures have dark beaks.

NATURAL DISTRIBUTION Australia, except coastal waters of New South Wales and Victoria.

HABITAT Open woods and grassy areas, arid interiors near water, in large flocks year round.

DIET Mixed millets, canary seed and greenfood.

SPECIAL NEEDS Don't breed females until 9 to 10 months old. Separate cocks and hens during winter, preferably indoors in unheated, frost-free area.

CAGE LIFE Adaptable, social, vivacious, hardy and easily tamed. Male has bright, vigorous trumpeting song. Good for all types of aviaries and large cages. Prolific breeders in outdoor aviaries, but limit to three per season to avoid egg binding and weak young. Remove all nesting materials (grass, plant fibres, feathers, wool), as soon as the nest is completed, to prevent further construction. The free nest is bottle-shaped, with an extrance tunnel. Likes to use all types of nest boxes. Lays 4 to 5 eggs, incubation, 13 to 16 days by both partners, fledging 20 to 22 days. Independent 3 weeks after it has flown out. Hang nest boxes near roof of cage or aviary to prevent birds from making another nest on top of it.

STATUS IN WILD Not listed as endangered.

Cut-Throat Finch

RIBBON FINCH
Amadina fasciata
ORDER Passeriformes FAMILY Estrildidae

DESCRIPTION 5 inches (12 to 13cm). Light tan, mottled with a black bar on each feather, grey-brown on tail and primaries. The male has a bright red band across its throat and cheeks.

NATURAL DISTRIBUTION Africa, south of Sahara, in three subspecies.

HABITAT Savannah, bush, farmland and near villages, in pairs during breeding, in sometimes large flocks other times. Broods in trees or deserted weaver and sparrow nests.

DIET Insects, sprouted seeds.

SPECIAL NEEDS Steady supply of minerals and cuttlefish bone since female susceptible to egg binding. Keep only with species of same size because they destroy nests of smaller birds.

CAGE LIFE Suitable for both large cages and aviaries. Good breeder, should limit to three broods per year. Uses half-open nest boxes, preferring dry grass, feathers, hay and wool. Lays 4 to 9 eggs, incubation 12 to 14 days, fledging 18 to 20 days, incubated and reared by both sexes.

STATUS IN WILD Not listed as endangered.

Cut-throat finch

Red-Headed Finch

RED-BROWED FINCH, PARADISE SPARROW
Amadina erythrocephala
ORDER Passeriformes FAMILY Estrildidae

DESCRIPTION 5¼ inches (13cm). Resembles Cut-Throat Finch – body light fawn, feathers marked with black bars, chocolate underside, grey tail, whitish throat with red band on front of neck – but male's entire head is dull red. Eyes brown, beak and legs pale. Female has a grey-brown head and duller underside.

NATURAL DISTRIBUTION South Africa, north through to Angola.

HABITAT Open country with bushes, in colonies. Broods in tree holes, deserted weaver or sparrow nests, or buildings.

DIET Seeds, insects.

SPECIAL NEEDS Seldom builds its own nests. Advisable to house single pair in separate, roomy aviary or breeding cage so they can breed successfully in peace.

CAGE LIFE Uses half-open nest boxes. Lays 3 to 6 eggs, incubation 12 to 13 days by both sexes; during day male sits longer than female, both parents at night. If disturbed, parents may start a nest somewhere else, leaving the young to die. After two weeks the young males already have red on their heads. Fledging 23 to 25 days. Young able to reproduce after six months, but breeding should be restricted until at least 1 year old. This species has hybridized with the Cut-Throat Finch, and the hybrids are fertile.

STATUS IN WILD Not listed as endangered.

Red-headed finch

Spice finch

Spice Finch

SPICE BIRD

Lonchura punctulata
ORDER Passeriformes FAMILY Estrildidae

DESCRIPTION 4½ inches (11cm). Spicy brown colour, darker brown on head, lighter brown and white on underparts and abdomen. Breast and flank feathers have dark brown edges. Young birds don't have characteristic scaly appearance. Male's beak thicker and heavier, head larger and broader.

NATURAL DISTRIBUTION India, Sri Lanka, south-eastern Asia, south China, Taiwan and Hainan, through Greater and Lesser Sundas (except Borney) to Sulawesi (formerly Celebes) and the Philippines; introduced into Australia, 1942–3.

HABITAT Grassland, parks and gardens.

DIET Seeds, insects.

SPECIAL NEEDS Hens have tendency to suffer from egg binding.

CAGE LIFE Appealing nature, easy to please. Aviary or glass enclosure. Male sings soft, almost inaudible song, detectable only by proud thrusts of head and puffing of throat feathers that accompany it. Almost always in motion. Can be brought into frost-free area in winter, but cannot tolerate temperate zones. Can spend winter outdoors if given aviary with sturdy night enclosure (containing felt-lined nest boxes, which also serve as sleeping places). Lays 4 to 7 (up to 10) white eggs, incubation 13 to 14 days by both parents, fledging 21 days.

STATUS IN WILD Not listed as endangered.

White-Headed Munia

MANNIKAN, NUN

Lonchura maja
ORDER Passeriformes   FAMILY Estrildidae

DESCRIPTION 5 inches (12cm). Chestnut-coloured body with white head, black underparts. Eyes brown, beak dark blue-grey, legs grey. Male's head sometimes brighter.

NATURAL DISTRIBUTION Malay Peninsula and neighbouring islands.

HABITAT Grassland, sometimes in very large flocks.

DIET Insects, cuttlebone, weed seeds, egg food, greens, canary-rearing food and stale bread soaked in milk or water.

SPECIAL NEEDS Its fast-growing nails should be carefully trimmed twice a year. Needs fresh bathwater daily. Will not tolerate scrutiny during the breeding cycle; supply with perches high up in aviary.

CAGE LIFE Much in demand around the world. Although the breeding results are only average, it is possible that a couple will breed if cage is in quiet and restful spot; better chance if male munia is mated with a Bengalese. Lays 4 to 5 eggs, incubation 12 to 13 days, fledging 20 to 21 days, but still fed by parents for a while.

STATUS IN WILD Not listed as endangered.

White-headed munia

Melba finch

Melba Finch

CRIMSON-FACED WAXBILL

Pytilia melba
ORDER Passeriformes FAMILY Estrildidae

DESCRIPTION 5 inches (12cm). Scarlet-orange forehead, chin and throat. Rest of head grey, underside grey with white streaks and spots. Olive chest, wings and back, blackish tail. Eyes brown, beak scarlet, legs brown. Hen duller, lacks red, has grey head.

NATURAL DISTRIBUTION Africa, south of the Sahara.

HABITAT Thorny thickets.

DIET Seeds, vitamins, minerals and, especially during breeding season, insects.

SPECIAL NEEDS Prevent pairs from throwing young out of nest by feeding rich variety of insects and small seeds. Usually aggressive towards other birds, so keep only one pair in community aviary.

CAGE LIFE Male has soft, sweet song. After acclimatization (at about 77°F/25°C, and no green foods for at least 3 weeks), can be housed in indoor, well-planted, sunny aviary. Outside aviary suitable only during hot summer months. Spends a lot of time on ground looking for small insects and spiders. Builds a little domed nest in small bush, seldom uses commercial nest box. Lays 3 to 4 eggs, incubation 12 days by both parents, fledging 20 to 21 days. Both parents rear, but often after 2 to 3 days throw their young out of the nest.

STATUS IN WILD Not listed as endangered.

Bicheno's Finch

DOUBLE-BARRED FINCH, OWL FINCH

Stizoptera (Poephila) bichenovii
ORDER Passeriformes FAMILY Estrildidae

DESCRIPTION 3 inches (8cm). Smallest of Australian grass-finches. Face, throat and underparts white with black bands across breast and neck. Forehead and front upperparts dark brown with fine bars, turning into light brown with fine bars, black wings with white dots, black tail and white rump. Eyes dark brown, beak grey, legs grey-brown. Female duller.

NATURAL DISTRIBUTION Eastern New South Wales, Queensland (except the southwestern parts), northern areas of Northern Territory, and northwestern Western Australia.

HABITAT Long grass and scrub, near water, and in cane fields, parks and gardens, in two subspecies.

DIET Insects, standard seed mixture. Drinks by sucking.

SPECIAL NEEDS House indoors in autumn and winter. Some live food throughout the year, especially during breeding season.

CAGE LIFE Friendly and peaceful aviary bird, often found on the ground. A leaf-mould compost heap in a corner will give them opportunity to look for insects, satisfying their urge for scratching. Builds own nest from grass and feathers in thick shrub or uses nest box. Breeding should be successful provided you have a true pair and aviary is not crowded. Lays 4 to 5 white eggs, incubation 14 days by both sexes, both sit on nest at night, fledging 22 days.

STATUS IN WILD Not listed as endangered.

Bicheno's finch

Strawberry Finch

RED AVADAVAT, TIGER FINCH

Amandava amandava
ORDER Passeriformes FAMILY Estrildidae

DESCRIPTION 4 inches (10cm). Reddish-brown with scarlet on sides of head, throat, underparts and rump, and black on tail. White spots on wings and tail coverts. Eyes brown, beak red, legs pink. Female reddish-brown with many white spots on the wings, uppertail coverts red, breast yellowish-grey. Male has seasonal change of plumage: during breeding season male is brown-red; at other times resembles female.

NATURAL DISTRIBUTION India, Pakistan, south Nepal, southeastern Asia, Moluccas and Indonesia. Also a variety in China with even more vivid red colouring.

HABITAT Scrub jungle and cultivated areas.

DIET Seeds, insects, live food.

SPECIAL NEEDS Can be quite troublesome towards other birds during the breeding period; house them separately at this time. Live food essential all year.

CAGE LIFE Male has clear-toned song all year round. Female also sings, particularly when without a mate, but not as well. During court-ship, male bursts into full swing, spreads tail feather and dances around female. Very suitable for breeding. Cock builds little nest in aviary or dense bush of long fibres, hair, feathers and grass. Lays 6 to 8 eggs, incubation 11 to 13 days by female while cock defends nest against intrusion, fledging 20 to 21 days. At fledging, beaks are still black; colouring begins to change at around 3 weeks and is completed by about 9 weeks but will not be retained until about 2 years of age.

STATUS IN WILD Not listed as endangered.

Strawberry finch

Golden-Breasted Waxbill

ZEBRA WAXBILL
Amandava subflava
ORDER Passeriformes FAMILY Estrildidae

DESCRIPTION 3½ inches (9cm). Olive-brown upperparts, yellow below, red rump, orange breast, red streak through eyes. Eyes brown, beak coral red, legs brown. Female duller.

NATURAL DISTRIBUTION Africa, south of the Sahara.

HABITAT Grassland and cultivated areas.

DIET Seeds, insects.

SPECIAL NEEDS May be aggressive towards other birds during breeding season, so provide enough plantlife for hiding places in aviary.

CAGE LIFE Keep in outside aviary in summer, in warmer area (around 64°F/18°C) in winter. Does not adapt easily to captivity and breeding results rare. May lay a few unfertilized eggs.

STATUS IN WILD Appendix 3.

Golden-breasted waxbill

Black-capped waxbill

Black-Capped Waxbill

Aegintha temporalis
ORDER Psittaciformes FAMILY Estrildidae

DESCRIPTION 4 inches (10cm). Mostly grey, darker above, with a prominent black cap, as well as black primaries and tail feathers, and red on rump and uppertail coverts.

NATURAL DISTRIBUTION South Africa.

HABITAT Forested areas. Usually in groups, sometimes quite large. Builds nests in tree branches.

DIET Seeds (particularly softer grass-type seeds), small insects.

SPECIAL NEEDS Outdoor, planted aviary, where the birds can catch their own live food, will enhance their lives and promote breeding. Must be kept warm at all times.

CAGE LIFE Can be quite tame, although always exhibits a lively, restless personality. Nest baskets are preferred over nest boxes. Lays 3 to 5 eggs, incubation time 12 days by both parents, fledging 28 days.

STATUS IN WILD Not listed as endangered.

Star Finch

Neochima (bathilda) ruficauda
ORDER Passeriformes   FAMILY Estrildidae

DESCRIPTION 4 to 4½ inches (10–11cm). Scarlet face with small white spots extending to and becoming larger on the light olive breast. Also light olive on back and wings. Uppertail coverts red, underparts pale yellow, tail rufous. Eyes brown, beak red, legs light brown. Female has less red, greyish underparts.

NATURAL DISTRIBUTION Northern Australia.

HABITAT Tall grass, rice fields, cane fields, bushes and trees, near water.

DIET Insects, seeds, greens and, especially during breeding season, vitamins, minerals and rearing foods.

SPECIAL NEEDS House indoors at room temperature during autumn and winter.

CAGE LIFE Peaceful, shy and quiet, good in aviary with other small finches. Spends a lot of time on ground. Male may become aggressive during breeding season. Easy to breed if kept in well-planted (grass, reeds, ivy, dense bushes), quiet aviary. Pair builds its own round grass nest, rather than use a box. Lays 3 to 5 eggs, incubation 13 to 14 days by both parents, fledging 22 to 25 days. Pair may throw young from nest when not satisfied with food.

STATUS IN WILD Not listed as endangered.

Star finch

Gouldian finch

Gouldian Finch

Chloebia gouldiae
ORDER Passeriformes FAMILY Estrildidae

DESCRIPTION 5½ inches (14cm). Scarlet head, bordered with narrow black band, followed by a broad turquoise band. Throat and chin black. Breast deep purple, followed by golden-yellow. Neck, wings and tail green. Undertail coverts white. Black tail. Eyes brown, beak white with smudges of red, legs pink tinted. Also black-headed form (most common in wild) and yellow-headed form (rare). Female duller and bill charcoal during season.

NATURAL DISTRIBUTION Northern Australia, especially Kimberley district.

HABITAT Grassy plains with trees, mangrove swamps and thickets, near water.

DIET Protein-rich foods, vitamins, minerals, soaked and just-sprouted small seeds. Avoid white millet as this causes illness and even death among Goulds.

SPECIAL NEEDS Dry, warm (86°F/30°C) aviary at humidity of about 70 per cent.

CAGE LIFE Social birds. Hollow log or half-open nest box 6 × 6 × 10 inches (15 × 15 × 25cm), entrance 2 inches (5cm), which they line with dry or fresh grass, hay or coconut fibre. Don't furnish materials longer than 4 inches (10cm). Some pairs prolific, others need Bengalese as foster parents. Lay 3 to 8 eggs, incubation 14 to 16 days by both partners, fledging 21 to 24 days. First moult at 8 to 10 weeks, adult colours at 5 months.

STATUS IN WILD Not listed as endangered.

Orange-Cheeked Waxbill

Estrilda melpoda
ORDER Passeriformes FAMILY Estrildidae

DESCRIPTION 4 inches (10cm). Body greyish-brown, with lighter, greyer crown and orange cheeks. Underside almost white, rump orangish, tail black. Eyes brown, beak red and legs pink. Hens may be paler and smaller. Immatures assume full plumage after first moult, which is approximately 7 weeks.

NATURAL DISTRIBUTION West and central Africa, in three subspecies, plus some in the Caribbean, where some escaped aviary birds established themselves.

HABITAT Grassland.

DIET Millet, plus various seeds.

SPECIAL NEEDS Insects (aphids, ant eggs and small mealworms) during rearing period.

CAGE LIFE Pleasing personalities. Prolific breeders, suitable for cage and aviary. Two males or two hens may act as a couple. Only the male sings. May be nervous. During breeding season, house in well-planted aviary, with low bushes and high grass; they like to construct nests about 5 feet (1.5m) from ground. Also use half-open nest boxes in which they build a ball-shaped structure. Lay 3 to 4, up to 7 white eggs, incubation 11 to 12 days, fledging 14 to 18 days. Both parents incubate and feed.

STATUS IN WILD Appendix 3.

Orange-cheeked waxbill

St Helena Waxbill

COMMON WAXBILL

Estrilda astrild
ORDER Passeriformes   FAMILY Estrildidae

DESCRIPTION 4½ inches (11.5cm). Body brown with dark bars on upperparts and abdomen, pinkish on underparts. Undertail coverts black. Crimson eye band over brown eyes and red beak. Female smaller with lighter markings and less pink on abdomen.

NATURAL DISTRIBUTION Africa, south of the Sahara; Madagascar, Mauritius, St Helena and New Caledonia; also feral in Portugal and parts of Spain; five subspecies.

HABITAT Grassland and cultivated areas.

DIET Millet, with various seeds.

SPECIAL NEEDS Live food during breeding season.

CAGE LIFE During breeding period, house just one pair in an aviary to avoid troubles. From grass and straw, cock builds bullet-shaped nest with false chamber. Will also use nest boxes, which should be hung high. Lays 1 to 4 white eggs, incubation 10 to 13 days by both parents, fledging 14 to 15 days, but parents feed for some time.

STATUS IN WILD Appendix 3.

St Helena waxbill

Red-eared waxbill

Red-Eared Waxbill

GREY WAXBILL, CORALBEAK
Estrilda troglodytes
ORDER Passeriformes FAMILY Estrildidae

DESCRIPTION 4 inches (10cm). Mouse-brown with some grey on head, highlighted by crimson eye line and beak. Underside and throat whitish with pink sheen. Tail black. Eyes and legs brown. During breeding season, male's red becomes more intense, and eyebrows become darker. He then displays, holding grass blade or other small object in his bill, dancing around the female.

NATURAL DISTRIBUTION Northern Africa from Senegal to Ethiopia.

HABITAT Semi-arid areas and swamps.

DIET Millet, with various seeds and live food.

SPECIAL NEEDS A lot of insect food and fresh bathing water daily. Must be kept indoors during winter.

CAGE LIFE Busy bird, with shrill song. At home in indoor and even in large outdoor aviaries. Towards end of summer, best housed in indoor aviary or large cage. Prefers to breed in garden aviaries with variety of nest boxes or builds bullet-shaped nests in hidden area. Lays 3 to 5 eggs, incubation 11 to 12 days, alternately by the male and female for 3 hours each, fledging 14 days, young take food from the parents for a while longer.

STATUS IN WILD Appendix 3.

Bengalese Finch

SOCIETY FINCH

Lonchura striata domestica
ORDER Passeriformes FAMILY Estrildidae

DESCRIPTION 5 inches (11cm). Bred in wide range of colours, and some varieties have small crest: dark brown are called Self Chocolate, lighter brown Self Fawns, pied variants Fawn and White, a Chestnut variant in self and pied forms, and pure called Self White. Immatures duller and paler. No visible distinction between sexes.

NATURAL DISTRIBUTION Not found in wild; bred from Sharp-Tailed Munia (*Lonchura striata*), and may have been first domesticated in China.

HABITAT Oldest-known domesticated cage bird.

DIET Millet and other small cereal seeds, plus greenstuff.

SPECIAL NEEDS Peace during breeding; do not disturb, even if known as a bird that allows regular nest inspections. Don't allow more than four broods per season, and avoid winter breeding.

CAGE LIFE Suitable as aviary and cage bird. Compatible and breeds readily. Male sings during breeding season. Supply with ample half-open nest boxes, 10 × 10 × 10 inches (25 × 25 × 25cm), and nesting material (coconut fibres and grass). Lays 5 to 7 eggs, incubation 18 to 21 days by both parents, fledging 20 to 24 days. Fed by parents for another 40 days, then move to large box cage. Young should not breed until at least 1 year old. Also excellent as foster parents. Return foster nestlings to natural parents once they reach adulthood; otherwise the young will want to stay near their foster parents and won't associate with own kind.

STATUS IN WILD Not listed as endangered.

Bengalese finch

African Silverbill

WARBLING SILVERBILL

Lonchura cantans
ORDER Passeriformes   FAMILY Estrildidae

DESCRIPTION 4½ inches (11cm). Sandy/taupe brown with subdued whitish stripes, darker on wings and tail, lighter on belly and undertail coverts. No visible distinction between sexes.

NATURAL DISTRIBUTION West and central Africa, in four subspecies.

HABITAT Savannahs, farmland and near villages, often nest under roofs, in walls of huts or in low shrubs.

DIET Greens, millet and especially spray millet as a treat.

SPECIAL NEEDS Do not disturb while breeding, even for nest control. Place in unheated area indoors during winter.

CAGE LIFE Male has soft musical song. Best breeding results in aviaries by themselves, but can also be placed in community aviaries or large cages. Lays 3 to 4 eggs, incubation 12 to 15 days by both sexes, fledging 21 days. Fifteen to 21 young in a season from one pair is common, but three broods per year produce best young and lower risk of egg binding. Also make suitable foster parents for finches that don't require insects.

STATUS IN WILD Not listed as endangered.

African silverbill

Java sparrow

Java Sparrow

RICE BIRD, PADDY BIRD, TEMPLE BIRD

Padda oryzivora
ORDER Passeriformes FAMILY Estrildidae

DESCRIPTION 5½ inches (14cm). Steel-blue body with black head and tail, white cheeks, pink eye ring and beak, which is very large. Eyes brown, legs flesh-coloured. Female smaller with narrower crown, more tapered and duller bill. Several mutations have been developed, including white, pied (calico) and brown or black-headed.

NATURAL DISTRIBUTION Java, Bali and neighbouring islands; introduced into Sri Lanka, southern Burma, Zanzibar, St Helena and other places.

HABITAT Rice and bamboo fields, in large flocks.

DIET Canary and millet seeds, millet sprays, green food and some soft food.

SPECIAL NEEDS Keeping Java sparrows in captivity is illegal in some parts of the United States because escaped birds could seriously threaten agriculture. If aviary is peaceful (only a few other inhabitants), may breed throughout the year, which could lead to egg-binding problems. Limit breeding period from May to July and no more than four clutches per season.

CAGE LIFE Ideal aviary inhabitants. Male stretches out neck and makes unusual bubbly noise. Prefer half-open nest boxes, 12 × 10 × 10 inches (30 × 25 × 25cm) or beechwood blocks, entrance diameter 2 inches (5cm). Do not hang too close together to avoid fighting. Lay 3 to 5 eggs, incubation 12 to 15 days, fledging 26 to 28 days.

STATUS IN WILD Not listed as endangered.

Diamond Sparrow

Stagonoplura guttata
ORDER Passeriformes FAMILY Estrildidae

DESCRIPTION 5 inches (13cm). Greyish-brown upperparts and wings, with grey face, black lores and black band across chest. Flanks black with white round spots, tail black and uppertail coverts red. Underparts and undertail coverts white. Eyes brown, beak red, legs grey-brown.

NATURAL DISTRIBUTION Eastern Australia.

HABITAT Woods, grassland, always near watercourses; usually in small groups, during breeding season in pairs. Often build nests in lower part of nests of birds of prey. They also build bullet-shaped free nests.

DIET Insects, seeds.

SPECIAL NEEDS Tend to get fat if kept in confined quarters; keep only one pair per well-planted aviary or large cage. Don't tolerate temperatures below 60°F (15°C); outside birds must be moved inside in autumn.

CAGE LIFE Often bully smaller birds or interfere with their nests, breaking their eggs or killing their young. Also advisable to let them choose their own partner. Provide with selection of nesting materials: coconut fibres, leaf veins, wool, moss and soft dry grass (up to 20 inches/50cm long), but avoid long, stringy parts which could cause entangling. Use various nest boxes or build free-standing bullet-shaped nests in thick bush. Lay 5 to 6 eggs, incubation 12 to 14 days by both parents, fledging 25 to 30 days. House independent young in separate flight to deter male from chasing them around.

STATUS IN WILD Not listed as endangered.

Diamond sparrow

Violet-Eared Waxbill

Granatina granatina
ORDER Passeriformes FAMILY Estrildidae

DESCRIPTION 4½ inches (11.5cm). Bright chestnut with violet ear patches, blue forehead and tail coverts and purple beak with red tip. Wings brownish-grey with red margins, tail has bluish edges. Chin, throat, vent and tail black. Eyes reddish-brown, legs greyish. Female duller, with greyish upperparts, yellowish underparts, whitish throat and no blue on undertail coverts.

NATURAL DISTRIBUTION Africa, from Angola to Zambia.

HABITAT Thorn scrub country and arid areas; in small flocks or pairs. Builds nest in thorny bushes.

DIET Small seeds (grass seeds, spray millet) plus live food throughout breeding season.

SPECIAL NEEDS Roomy aviary, and will not survive in temperatures below 70–77°F (21–25°C).

CAGE LIFE Generally friendly, can be hostile and aggressive towards members of same genus. Lays 3 to 6 white eggs, incubation 13 to 15 days by both parents, fledging 17 to 18 days.

STATUS IN WILD Not listed as endangered.

Violet-eared waxbill

Red-Cheeked Cordon Bleu

Uraeginthus bengalus
ORDER Passeriformes FAMILY Estrildidae

DESCRIPTION 4½ to 5 inches (11.5 to 12.5cm). Mousey upperparts and abdomen blended with sky blue on face, throat, breast, uppertail coverts and sides. Accented by crimson ear patches and beak with black tip. Tail a duller blue. Eyes brown, legs yellowish-brown. Female lacks the ear patches, appear on young males after about 5 months.

NATURAL DISTRIBUTION Africa, from Senegal to Ethiopia and south from eastern Africa to Zambia.

HABITAT Open country and cultivated areas.

DIET Live food (ant eggs, aphids and spiders), especially during breeding season.

SPECIAL NEEDS Towards end of summer, best housed in indoor aviary or large cage. Imported birds must be carefully acclimatized; a warm (77°F/25°C) indoor and roomy aviary or large cage is essential.

CAGE LIFE Lively aviary bird. Prefers to breed in garden aviaries with thick plantings and variety of nest boxes. Builds oven-shaped nests of fine grasses and feathers, but also accepts half-open nest boxes. Lays 4 to 5 white eggs, incubation 11 to 13 days by both partners, fledging 17 days. Breeds all year, but best to allow only two broods, during May and September.

STATUS IN WILD Appendix 3.

Chinese Painted Quail

PAINTED QUAIL, BLUE-BREASTED QUAIL
Excalfactoria chinensis
ORDER Galliformes FAMILY Phasianidae

DESCRIPTION 4½ inches (11.5cm). White cheeks with black border, throat black. Broad white band across upper breast and sides of neck. Chest and flanks bluish-grey. Lower chest and underparts deep chocolate brown. Eyes hazel, beak black and legs yellow. Hen lacks black and white markings and blue-grey on chest and flanks. Immatures resemble parents after two months.

NATURAL DISTRIBUTION India and southern China.

HABITAT Swamps and grassland.

DIET Heavy rations of live insects. During rearing, eggs and rusk, soaked bread, commercial rearing food, ant pupae, poppy seed and green food.

SPECIAL NEEDS Like most quail, has habit of flying vertically when alarmed; install layer of sacking just under roof mesh and meshed netting just below that. Also may need more than one hen with a cock for breeding. If kept with other birds, cover drinking vessel to prevent soiling with droppings. Also, don't place food and water containers near walls because quail tend to run along edges of habitat. Don't keep two pairs in same place as you risk the cocks fighting to the death.

CAGE LIFE One of the most pleasant and frequently imported species. Builds nest on ground, often with low wall or roof to protect from elements. Lays 4 to 12 grey-olive or olive-brown eggs with black stripes and spots, behind low clumps of plants, incubation 16 days only by female. Independent at about 6 weeks. Place panels of glass, board or cardboard around bottom edge of aviary so small hatchlings cannot slip through. Also provide drinking water in container too shallow to do harm to chicks that might fall in. Hen will begin second clutch when young become independent. Remove original brood to brood machine or place in aquarium tank warmed with heat lamp.

STATUS IN WILD Not listed as endangered.

Chinese painted quail

Common Peafowl

INDIAN PEAFOWL, PEACOCK

Pavo cristatus
ORDER Galliformes   FAMILY Phasianidae

DESCRIPTION 78¾ to 90 inches (200 to 229cm). Male known for its long train consisting of elongated uppertail coverts that can be spread into dazzling fan by raising tail beneath. Neck and breast deep bright blue, lower back bronze-green with scallops and uppertail coverts bronze-green with purplish and black in centre, rump black. Copper-coloured eyes, face white and black, fan-shaped crest of wiry feathers. Female 34 inches (86cm). Head crested as male and nape rufous brown, upperparts brown, mottled paler; primaries brown; lower neck metallic green, breast buff glossed green, belly buffy white. Legs and bill grey, eyes brown. Immature male resembles female, but primaries chestnut.

NATURAL DISTRIBUTION Sri Lanka, India, Pakistan, Himalayas; introduced worldwide.

HABITAT Deciduous forests and semi-open country flanking hillside streams, with thick undergrowth and thorny creepers. Also forages farmland, particularly dense, tall crops such as sugar cane. Travels in small parties of males and 3 to 5 females when nesting, but sexes segregate after breeding. Feeds and drinks in open early and late, prefaced by crowing; also stimulated by thunder. Roosts in tall trees.

DIET Seeds, grain, lentils, ground nuts, green crops.

SPECIAL NEEDS Shelter as well as outside habitat.

CAGE LIFE Male screams and repeats head movements, raising train, quivering drooped wings, strutting, prancing and presenting back view. Female occasionally responds. Rests during day in thickets, runs to escape, seldom taking wing, rockets upward with loud flaps.

STATUS IN WILD Not listed as endangered.

Common peafowl

Helmeted Guineafowl

Numida mitrata
ORDER Galliformes FAMILY Numididae

DESCRIPTION 21 to 22¾ inches (53 to 58cm). Distinguished by bony casque (the helmet) atop its head covered with a sheath of keratin and very well-developed blue and/or red wattles.

NATURAL DISTRIBUTION Eastern Chad to Ethiopia, east to Rift Valley, south to borders of northern Zaire, northern Kenya and Uganda. Has been domesticated around the world as food species.

HABITAT Open grassland. Outside breeding season, may forage in flocks of several hundred, and have been known to gather in numbers around 2,000. During breeding, split up into monogamous pairs.

DIET Bulbs, tubers, berries, insects and snails.

SPECIAL NEEDS Shelter as well as outside habitat.

CAGE LIFE Lays 6 to 19 eggs in scrape on the ground, incubation by female.

STATUS IN WILD Not listed as endangered.

Helmeted guinea fowl

Great Argus Pheasant

Argusianus argus
ORDER Galliformes FAMILY Phasianidae

DESCRIPTION 80 inches (203cm). Distinguishing feature is tremendous tail, from plumage showing complicated pattern of chestnut, brown, white, black and grey spots, ocelli and bars. Female up to 30 inches (76cm).

NATURAL DISTRIBUTION Indo-China, Malaysia, Borneo, Sumatra, Thailand.

HABITAT Lowland and hill forest.

DIET Fallen fruits, ants, slugs and snails; meat, insects and fruit especially during breeding.

SPECIAL NEEDS Cannot stand frost, must be well sheltered.

CAGE LIFE Male clears display site in forest away from his rivals, attracts female with calls and dances before her. At the climax, he fans his wing feathers. If female is impressed, she consents to mating. Female lays 2 eggs and rears chicks alone, while male courts other females. Both sexes solitary.

STATUS IN WILD Appendix 2.

Argus pheasant

Golden pheasant

Golden Pheasant

Chrysolophus pictus
ORDER Galliformes FAMILY Phasianidae

DESCRIPTION 40 to 44 inches (102 to 112cm), with tail 32 inches (81cm). Upper back dark green, feathers edged black; lower back and rump 'silky'; crown and crest golden yellow; short, rounded wings with dark brown primaries, chestnut and black secondaries, deep blue tertiaries; long central curved tail feathers black, spotted cinnamon; tips of tail coverts scarlet; ruff light orange barred black, underparts scarlet; legs (with short spurs), bill horn yellow, eyes and facial skin light yellow. Female 25 to 27 inches (63.5 to 68.5cm), with tail 14 to 15 inches (35.5 to 38cm) mixed brown with black streaks, spots and bars. Legs, bill horn yellow, eyes brown, face red.

NATURAL DISTRIBUTION Central China; introduced to Britain.

HABITAT Rocky hills covered with bamboo and other scrub.

DIET Seeds, leaves, tender shoots (bamboos); insects.

SPECIAL NEEDS Shelter as well as outside habitat.

CAGE LIFE Solitary or in pairs. Reluctant to fly. During courtship male raises crest and spreads ruff, trails a wing towards female, opens tail vertically, jumps from side to side of female, whistling and clicking. Breeds probably in May and June in wild, nesting on ground. Lays 8 pale buff to cream eggs, incubation 22 days by female, male may help with brood.

STATUS IN WILD Not listed as endangered.

Silver pheasant

Silver Pheasant

Lophura nycthemera
ORDER Galliformes FAMILY Phasianidae

DESCRIPTION Male 35½ to 50 inches (90 to 127cm). Long white tail, red face, long black crest. Upperparts white, lined with black. Yellow bill, red legs. Female 21¾ to 26¾ inches (55 to 68cm), earthy brown, streaked with whitish below. First-year males brown, larger and lighter than females, more bars on breast and tail.

NATURAL DISTRIBUTION Southern China, eastern Burma, Indo-China, Hainan.

HABITAT Grassland bordered by forest, rarely penetrates into dense forest.

DIET Range of animal and vegetable matter, including beetles, flower petals, grass and leaves.

SPECIAL NEEDS Shelter as well as outside habitat.

CAGE LIFE Polygamous, like most grassland pheasants, with dominant males courting many females and defending their territory with whistling calls. Several hens can be kept with one cock. Does well at liberty, but a poor game bird because it seldom flies.

STATUS IN WILD Not listed as endangered.

Lady Amherst's Pheasant

Chrysolophus amherstiae
ORDER Galliformes FAMILY Phasianidae

DESCRIPTION 52 to 68 inches (132 to 173cm), with tail 34 to 46 inches (86 to 117cm). Blue-green mantle and scapulars, yellow back and orange rump. Central tail feathers white barred in black, wings shiny blue, neck ruff white with dark blue margins. Head dark green with red crest. Underparts white to black undertail coverts; legs and bill bluish grey, eyes yellow, face white. Female 26 to 27 inches (66 to 68.5cm), with tail 12 to 15 inches (30 to 38cm), like Golden Pheasant but more rufous and striking black, tail feathers rounded and eyes brown to yellow.

NATURAL DISTRIBUTION Tibet, China and Burma; introduced to Britain.

HABITAT Thickets, especially bamboo, in rocky mountains, and in woods and scrub. Flocks of 20 to 30 through winter. Flies more readily than Golden Pheasant.

DIET Bamboo shoots and small animals, including spiders, earwigs and beetles. Seen feeding in shallow flowing water, turning over stones for aquatic animals.

SPECIAL NEEDS Shelter as well as outside habitat.

CAGE LIFE Most elusive of true pheasants, rarely emerges from thickets of habitat. Wild population breeds in dense woodland with thick undergrowth. Lays 6 to 8 buff cream eggs, incubation 23 days by female, who hardly ever leaves nest.

STATUS IN WILD Not listed as endangered.

Lady Amherst's pheasant

Reeve's Pheasant

Syrmaticus reevesi
ORDER Galliformes FAMILY Phasianidae

DESCRIPTION Short body with tremendously long tail. Head and neck white, with black band from bill to nape. Body colour yellow and well marked with buff, brown, grey and black.

NATURAL DISTRIBUTION Central and western China.

HABITAT Suitable game bird to introduce into forested and hilly country.

DIET Insects, seeds.

SPECIAL NEEDS Shelter as well as outside habitat. Better to keep two or three hens with one cock.

CAGE LIFE Strong and hardy. Usually breeds second year. Lays 7 to 15 olive-brown eggs, incubation 24 to 25 days.

STATUS IN WILD Not listed as endangered.

Reeve's pheasant

Red-legged partridge

Red-Legged Partridge

Salectoris rufa
ORDER Galliformes FAMILY Phasianidae

DESCRIPTION 13½ inches (34cm). Upperparts mouse brown fading to buff belly, grey throat and forehead, white cheeks and over eye, and on throat bordered with black. Short tail rufous; flanks grey, barred black, white, chestnut. Legs and bill red, eyes brown.

NATURAL DISTRIBUTION Southwest Europe, mainly France and Iberia; introduced into Britain, Azotes, Madeira, Canary Islands.

HABITAT Lowland scrub, sunny hillsides, vineyards, heaths; in England on drier cultivated land and dunes.

DIET Stems, leaves, buds, berries, grass seeds, insects and spiders.

SPECIAL NEEDS Runs rather than flies; coveys scatter if put to flight.

CAGE LIFE Uses call when about to fly. Often perches at height. Breeds from mid-April, lining well-hidden scrape with grass and leaves. Lays 10 to 16 eggs, pale yellow brown, spotted dull red and ashy. Sometimes lays in nests of other birds. Often two clutches, each parent incubating one 23 to 24 days. Young attended by one or both parents, fledging 16 weeks.

STATUS IN WILD Not listed as endangered.

Barbary Dove

BLOND RINGDOVE, RINGDOVE, DOMESTIC RINGDOVE, DOMESTIC COLLARED DOVE, FAWN DOVE

Streptopelia risoria
ORDER Columbiformes   FAMILY Columbidae

DESCRIPTION 9 inches (23cm). Light fawn with pinkish on breast and black ring around back of neck. Eyes yellow, beak orange, legs pink. Males paler than females, but degree is variable. Domesticated form of African collared dove (*S. roseogrisa*). A white variety is called 'Java dove'; majority of Barbary carry white in genetic make-up, so may produce white offspring. There are also apricot varieties and frilled forms, both recessive.

NATURAL DISTRIBUTION Domesticated; also a 'wild' colony in Los Angeles, California.

HABITAT More suitable for aviary than cage.

DIET Canary and millet seeds and mixtures for domestic pigeon. Basic maintenance diet until breeding period, when protein should be increased. Grit, plus cuttlefish bone, should always be available; may take greenstuff, particularly young leafy plants such as chickweed. When breeding they may prefer to use leafy greens for nesting material. To avoid, cut greenstuff into pieces. Ingest seeds directly; do not dehusk. Drink by active sucking rather than passive swallowing. Prefer to feed off floor.

SPECIAL NEEDS During winter house indoors at approximately 50°F (10°C).

CAGE LIFE Often tame enough to perch freely on hand. Friendly, even towards small finches and such, but can be aggressive to males of own species. Extremely free-breeding, may nest on floor in corner of cage. Cage approximately 5 feet (1.5m) long, 23½ inches (60cm) deep, and 35½ inches (90cm) high. Allow daily exercise in room. For nesting, supply tray, 8 × 4 inches (20 × 10cm) and a few inches high, or flat basket, and materials such as twigs and straw. Lays 2 white eggs, anywhere in aviary if no breeding places provided, incubation 14 days.

STATUS IN WILD Not listed as endangered.

Barbary dove

Diamond Dove

Geopelia cuneata
ORDER Columbiformes FAMILY Columbidae

DESCRIPTION 7½ to 8¾ inches (19 to 22cm). Greyish-brown with white dots on wings, lighter grey on head and underside, pale beak and red eye ring. Female smaller with browner plumage and more and larger wing spots. Cock is the one that spreads the long, pointed tail. Immatures achieve adult colouring at 1 month, fully coloured eye-ring at 2 months.

NATURAL DISTRIBUTION Australia, but in east and south only after irregular coastward movements during dry periods.

HABITAT Dry woodland and scrub.

DIET Mix of canary-grass seeds (25 per cent), white millet (25 per cent), red millet (20 per cent), niger-thistle seed (10 per cent), sesame seed (10 per cent), wheat (5 per cent) and poppy (5 per cent). When young arrive, also offer universal food, rearing food, small mealworms and ant pupae (preferably fresh). Feeds on the ground.

SPECIAL NEEDS Bring indoors during winter, at not less than 48°F (9°C); also separate cocks and hens to avoid exhaustion from continuous breeding; limit clutches to 4 or 5 per season.

CAGE LIFE Lively, yet peaceful and easy to care for. Not aggressive to smaller birds, can be a nuisance when kept individually so advisable to keep in pair. Requires sunny cage or aviary to enjoy sunbathing. In aviary, place a gauze 'nest', filled with twigs and grass. In breeding cage 40 × 32 inches (102 × 81cm), place box or tray. Male courting display includes bowing with tail raised and fanned. Lays 2 to 3 white eggs, incubation 13 days by both male and female, fledging 10 to 14 days. Parents continue feeding for some time; remove as soon as young eat independently or they may be attacked and even killed by parents.

STATUS IN WILD Not listed as endangered.

Diamond dove

Red-Vented Bulbul

Pycnonotus cafer
ORDER Passeriformes FAMILY Pycnonotidae

DESCRIPTION 8 to 8½ inches (20 to 21cm). Black head and throat, blending with brown on neck, shoulders, breast and wings, highlighted with white. Flanks and underside greyish, grey back shades to white. Undertail coverts reddish, tail brown with white tips. Brown cheeks and eyes, beak and legs blackish. Female smaller and duller, beak larger and slimmer.

NATURAL DISTRIBUTION India and Southeast Asia.

HABITAT Farmland, near villages, up to 5,600 feet (1,700m) in the mountains, in small groups in the winter.

DIET Fruit, softbill food or mynah pellets and some live food.

SPECIAL NEEDS House indoors in lightly heated area in winter.

CAGE LIFE Tolerant of other species if kept as singles. Raises head feather into crest, spreads reddish undertail feathers and may sing, especially when excited. Female responds by lowering crest and dropping wings. House in cage 31½ × 19¾ × 19¾ inches (80 × 50 × 50cm), cup-shaped nest filled with moss, hay, grass and coconut fibres. Lays 3 to 4 white eggs with red background and purplish markings at one end, incubation 12 to 14 days by female, fledging 12 to 14 days.

STATUS IN WILD Not listed as endangered.

Red-vented bulbul

White-Eared Bulbul

YELLOW-VENTED BULBUL

Pycnonotus leucotis
ORDER Passeriformes FAMILY Pycnonotidae

DESCRIPTION 7 inches (18cm). White neck, breast sides and bell, darker greyish-brown on top, yellowish at vent.

NATURAL DISTRIBUTION Iran to West Pakistan.

HABITAT Often in large groups, in wooded areas near water, and often near people in winter. Can damage fruit crops. Builds nest in thick bush.

DIET Fruit, softbill food, mynah pellets, live food.

SPECIAL NEEDS Intolerant of cold; house indoors in lightly heated area during winter.

CAGE LIFE Lively, inquisitive, tame. Normally pleasant, but during breeding season can be destructive, and may interfere with nests of other birds. House in densely planted flight, free cup-shaped nest. Lays 2 to 4 whitish eggs with red blotches, dots and stripes. Incubation 12 to 13 days by female, male will feed, fledging 14 to 17 days.

STATUS IN WILD Not listed as endangered.

White-eared bulbul

Golden-Fronted Leafbird

FRUITSUCKER

Chloropsis aurifrons
ORDER Passeriformes FAMILY Irenidae

DESCRIPTION 8 inches (20cm). Dark green body, underside and tail bright grass-green, accented by black eye band circling through cheeks and neck to breast under blue throat, yellow crown, blue wing curve and brownish flight feathers. Eyes brown, beak black, legs steel blue. Female duller.

NATURAL DISTRIBUTION Himalayan region in India and Indo-China; Burma and Sumatra.

HABITAT Forest, scrub.

DIET Fruit, nectar, insectile mixture, live food.

SPECIAL NEEDS Moults in autumn and dislikes cold, damp weather and fluctuating temperatures; move inside about 64°F (18°C) before winter weather develops. Always introduce pair to quarters together.

CAGE LIFE Cage or aviary bird, sings beautifully, enjoys bathing. Drinks a lot and makes mess at feeding dishes by inspecting contents piece by piece. Quick-tempered, and can be aggressive towards other birds. Cage 31½ × 20 × 24 inches (80 × 50 × 60cm). Spends most of time in trees and bushes, flies very little. Cup-shaped nest of moss, hair, stalks, leaves, long grass, hay, spider webs, coconut and hemp fibres; lined with small roots and moss; placed in fork of branch. Lays 2 to 3 reddish-white eggs with spots, circles and small stripes. Incubation 14 to 16 days, fledging 17 to 18 days.

STATUS IN WILD Not listed as endangered.

Golden-fronted leafbird

Pekin robin

Pekin Robin

RED-BILLED LEIOTHRIX,
JAPANESE NIGHTINGALE

Leiothrix lutea
ORDER Passeriformes FAMILY Timaliidae

DESCRIPTION 6 inches (15cm). Greenish-grey head, neck, upperbody, wing coverts, small flight feathers and uppertail coverts. Red flight feathers with black and yellow bands, yellow throat blending to orange chest, black top of tail, beige stripe by eye. Eyes brown, beak red with black, legs brownish. Female's head is duller. Fledging young approximately one-third larger than parents because they carry extra fat until become more active. Immatures have pinkish-red bill and more grey and black in plumage, achieve colouring by 70 or 80 days.

NATURAL DISTRIBUTION From south Himalayas across northern Indo-China and China.

HABITAT Heavily wooded areas, starting at 19,685 feet (6,000m) above sea level, most abundant below 6,560 feet (2,000m), usually in groups, in pairs during breeding period.

DIET Mealworm, ant pupae, millet, canary-grass seed, maw seed, hemp, chopped boiled egg, berries, banana slices, chopped apple or pear, soaked raisins, soaked stale bread and grit, lettuce, spinach, chickweed.

SPECIAL NEEDS Keeping more than one pair in cage or aviary leads to fighting. Feeding mealworms during nesting and breeding may result in birds' throwing their eggs or young out of the nest and starting again.

CAGE LIFE Strong, lively, beautiful song accompanied in male by wing-flapping display. Can be kept with seed-eaters, but may plunder nests. Male and female act very 'lovingly' towards each other. When excited, male repeats 'terr' call almost constantly, and female has softer call. Cage 30 × 18 × 25½ inches (75 × 45 × 65cm). Use canary 'baskets', placed in half-open nest boxes, or build cup-shaped nest of straw, bark, moss, thin roots and twigs. Nest box should be hung in secluded location. Need daily access to bathing water warmed to room temperature. May remain outside in winter if heatable night shelter keeps them wind- and rain-free. Breed April to June. Lay 3 to 5 pale green-white eggs with markings at blunt end, incubation 13 to 14 days, fledging 11 to 13 days, fed by parents for some time.

STATUS IN WILD Not listed as endangered.

Silver-Eared Mesia

Leiothrix argentauris
ORDER Passeriformes FAMILY Timaliidae

DESCRIPTION 7 inches (18cm). Orange-yellow underparts, blending into red throat, rump and undertail. Yellow on brown folded wing, mantle olive with red, black crown. Legs brownish, beak yellow, eyes red. Female lacks red throat and rump, is duller on yellow.

NATURAL DISTRIBUTION Eastern Nepal through Indo–China to Sumatra.

HABITAT Mountain forests, except in winter, when it descends to lower terrain, joining other birds. Flocks up to 10, feeding on insects or fruit near ground.

DIET Mealworm, ant pupae, millet, canary-grass seed, maw seed, hemp, chopped boiled egg, berries, banana slices, chopped apple or pear, soaked raisins, soaked stale bread and grit, lettuce, spinach, chickweed.

SPECIAL NEEDS Male's full, deep call and song too loud for indoors.

CAGE LIFE Good breeder, generally tolerant of other birds in large community aviary. Pair builds free cup-shaped nest together, between twigs, preferably in thick small bushes or shrubs. Line with dry bamboo leaves, roots (prefers coloured ones) and moss. In aviary, also uses canary 'string nests' with coconut fibres, roots and maybe bamboo leaves. Breeds April to August. Lays 3 to 4 light green-blue eggs with red-brown and brown markings mostly at blunt end. Incubation 14 days by both parents, mainly female, fledging 13 to 14 days.

STATUS IN WILD Not listed as endangered.

Silver-eared mesia

Indian white-eyed zosterops

Indian White-Eyed Zosterops

ORIENTAL ZOSTEROPS, INDIAN WHITE-EYE
Zosterops palpebrosa
ORDER Passeriformes FAMILY Zosteropidae

DESCRIPTION 4 to 6 inches (10 to 14cm). Named for the bold circle of white feathers around the eye. Olive on top, head and neck, becoming paler at sides and blending into bright yellow under-side and greyish stomach. Eyes brown, beak black, legs greyish. Immatures greener and duller, white around eyes.

NATURAL DISTRIBUTION India, Sri Lanka, Indo-China and the Greater Sunda Islands.

HABITAT Lowland woods, but can also be found at high altitudes. Leave for breeding grounds in April.

DIET Place food on small table of some sort, approximately 16 to 24 inches (40 to 60cm) be-cause they are rarely on the ground; are usually in foliage looking for insects, larvae, berries, fruit, leafbuds and even nectar drawn with their pointed beak. Also like soaked or cooked rice, berries, bilberries, bananas, dried fruits; mashed-fruit concoction of cherries, apples, pears, apricots, oranges and dates sweetened with fruit sugar; and mixture of small ant pupae, sponge cake and grated apples and carrots.

SPECIAL NEEDS Low tolerance of temperature changes and low temperatures; preferable to keep indoors in winter. Bathing an absolute must. Slowly pine away if not kept in pairs.

CAGE LIFE Tolerant towards other species, ex-tremely tame with keeper. Male has pleasant song. Show to full advantage in glass area or cage 27½ × 20 × 24 inches (70 × 50 × 60cm). Build shallow, cup-shaped nest in trees and thick bushes of moss and plant fibres. Lay 2 to 4 green-blue eggs, incubation 10 to 12 days by both par-ents, fledging 10 to 13 days. Separate young as soon as become independent to avoid father chas-ing them aggressively. Nest never used again, and is sometimes partially destroyed and materials re-used.

STATUS IN WILD Not listed as endangered.

Greater Hill Mynah

HILL MYNAH BIRD
Gracula religiosa
ORDER Passeriformes FAMILY Sturnidae

DESCRIPTION 10 to 18 inches (25 to 45cm). Body black with metallic sheen on back; beak orange, lighter at tip. Flights black, marked with white. Back of eyes and ear coverts covered by folds of bare, yellow skin. Eyes, feet and legs dark. No visible distinction between sexes. Immatures duller, and lack wattles on head.

NATURAL DISTRIBUTION India, through Southeast Asia and Indonesia; introduced elsewhere.

HABITAT Woods and forests, near water, in large groups.

DIET Softbill food or pellets, plus fruit and live food, such as mealworms; standard insectivorous; also dried fruits, such as currants, raisins, sultanas and dates. Young birds sometimes called 'gapers' because they solicit hand-feeding by gaping with open beaks.

SPECIAL NEEDS Daily bathing, preferably in the morning in something the size of a dog bowl made of earthenware, keeps plumage clean; screen portion of cage near bath with sheet of clear plastic to prevent soaking of surrounding areas. Well-balanced diet with vitamins and minerals, as well as much sunlight, to avoid convulsions similar to human epileptic seizures. Change newspaper in cage at least once a day, and regularly wash down perches. Keep in even temperature, especially when older and during winter, to avoid chills and respiratory problems.

CAGE LIFE Although other species are known as mynahs, Greater Hill's powers of mimicry are superior. Words repeated by this species are clearer than those of parrots. If kept in aviaries and not trained to mimic human speech, they repeat whatever sounds they are exposed to. Cage 35½ × 22 × 22 inches (90 × 55 × 55cm), of stainless steel or galvanized metal, with false wire bottom. Supply cockatiel or starling nest box all

year; in breeding season supply dry leaves, hay, straw, twigs, coconut and hemp fibres as building material. Lays 2 to 4 green-blue eggs with brown spots, incubation 14 to 15 days by both parents, fledging 4 to 5 weeks, independent at 8 to 10 weeks. Elderly birds may lose feathers that will not be replaced.

STATUS IN WILD Not listed as endangered.

Greater hill mynah

Superb Spreo Starling

Lamprotornis or *Spreo superbus*
ORDER Passeriformes   FAMILY Sturnidae

DESCRIPTION 8 inches (20cm). Colour metallic blue-green, head black, wings green with plush black spots, reddish underparts with white border, white on undertail coverts, axilliaries and underwing. Grey legs and bill, eyes yellowish. Immatures dull black on head, neck and upperparts.

NATURAL DISTRIBUTION Somalia, Ethiopia, Sudan, East Africa.

HABITAT Thornbush and acacia country, near habitations.

DIET Fruits, live foods.

SPECIAL NEEDS Since breeds readily in aviary, remove young of first brood when second is started.

CAGE LIFE Chattering call, loud alarm, whistling song, imitates other birds. In courting jumps with wings behind and neck extended. Breeding season varies. Nest of twigs, grass, feathers, low in tree or bush. In captivity roomy parakeet nest boxes or old thrush nests. Lays 3 to 4 blue-green eggs with bright reddish-brown or blue spots, incubation 14 to 15 days, fledging 25 days.

STATUS IN WILD Not listed as endangered.

Superb spreo starling

Shama Thrush

INDIAN NIGHTINGALE
Copsychus malabaricus
ORDER Passeriformes FAMILY Turdidae

DESCRIPTION 9 to 11 inches (23 to 28cm). Body bluish-black with white on rump and sides of tail. Underparts bold chestnut, beak black, eyes blackish-brown and feet and legs deep yellow. In female, black areas are greyish-brown and chestnut is ruddy fawn.

NATURAL DISTRIBUTION India, and Indo-China, with 20 subspecies in Sri Lanka, Burma, Thailand, China and Malaysia.

HABITAT Nests in holes and cracks, especially in bamboo.

DIET Egg, caterpillars (without hair), raw minced beef, universal food, thrush food, earthworms, grasshoppers, beetles and white worms. Also insects during rearing.

SPECIAL NEEDS Separate pair from other birds if plan to breed.

CAGE LIFE Pleasant with attractive voice, adept at imitating thrush and nightingale songs, as well as other noises such as creaking. Once acclimatized, can spend winter in draft-free aviary if night shelter provided. Aviary should have sufficient hiding places like shrubbery and undergrowth because hen withdraws during breeding cycle to avoid pursuing male. Nest cup-shaped, prefers lining of moss, hair, hemp fibres, twigs and small pieces of fabric. Lays 3 to 6 eggs in varied blues and greens with brown markings, incubation 11 to 12 days mainly by female, fledging 12 to 13 days, able to eat without hen after about 30 days. Once ready to fly, confine parents from joining them in freedom.

STATUS IN WILD Not listed as endangered.

Shama thrush

Paradise Tanager

Tangara chilensis
ORDER Passeriformes FAMILY Thraupidae

DESCRIPTION 5 inches (13cm). Black neck, shoulders, back and tail, accented by brilliant sky blue on breast, belly (with black in centre) and wing coverts; yellowish-green head; purple-edged wings; and red or yellow-red rump. Eyes brown, beak and legs black.

NATURAL DISTRIBUTION South America, east of the Andes and south to Bolivia and southern Brazil.

HABITAT Forests and woodland, up to about 4,921 feet (1,500m) elevation.

DIET Fruit, insects.

SPECIAL NEEDS Cover bottom of cage with absorbent paper towels or layers of newspaper to soak up watery dropping caused by their sweet, juicy diet. Clean daily to avoid spread of disease.

CAGE LIFE Large, well-planted aviary or cage at least 59¼ × 31½ × 23½ inches (150 × 80 × 60cm), with washing facilities. Breeding results sporadic in captivity. Prefers to breed as high as possible in variety of nest boxes containing coconut fibres, dead and live grass, leaves, moss, pieces of bark, wool and other materials. Likes to hide in corners on ground, may build nest free in thick shrub. Lays 2 to 3 eggs, incubation 13 to 14 days.

STATUS IN WILD Not listed as endangered.

Paradise tanager

Superb Tanager

ORANGE-RUMPED TANAGER

Tangara fastuosa
ORDER Passeriformes FAMILY Thraupidae

DESCRIPTION 5½ inches (14cm). Overall black with purple-blue sheen on shoulders and tail, and a 'ski-mask' hood of bluish-green with eye and beak area showing through black. Rump and underside orange, lesser wing coverts blue-green. Eyes brown, beak and legs black. Female has the hood effect on head, but other colouring duller. Immatures achieve adult plumage after about a year.

NATURAL DISTRIBUTION East Brazil.

HABITAT Forests, high in the crowns of trees, leaving only to seek food, in small groups.

DIET Variety of fruit – berries, currants, raisins, grapes, cut pear, apple, dates, figs, bananas, halved oranges – as well as rusk crumbs, ant pupae, small mealworms, grated carrots, chopped boiled egg and fatless red meat. For a treat, bread soaked in milk and honey.

SPECIAL NEEDS Keep recently imported birds at constant 77°F (25°C), gradually decreasing to 68°F (20°C) after acclimatization. Hose down daily and provide with room-temperature bath water. Allow to breed only in habitat without small exotic birds because they may steal young birds from the nests.

CAGE LIFE Tame and tolerant birds for cage or aviary. If kept in cage, cover bottom, but not with sand; supply shell grit separately. In aviary, like to hide and chase each other. Prefer to live in small groups, so keep a few pairs together. Allow to fly in room with cage, preferably towards evening. Pair builds nest together, as high as possible. Lay 2 to 4 pinkish-red eggs with darker spots, incubation 13 to 14 days, fledging 14 to 21 days.

STATUS IN WILD Not listed as endangered.

Cuvier's Toucan

Ramphastos cuvieri
ORDER Piciformes FAMILY Ramphastidae

DESCRIPTION 18 inches (45cm). Body black with white around eyes and down breast, bordered in red. Undertail red with yellow accent, and beak black with yellow border on top and around area near face.

NATURAL DISTRIBUTION Northern South America, where they are hunted for their tasty dark meat.

HABITAT Tropical rain forests, at low and middle altitudes.

DIET Fresh and dried fruit, with some coarse insectivorous and possibly an occasional young bird or egg, white bread or soaked rice. Tosses food into air before swallowing and is adept at catching.

SPECIAL NEEDS Be sure diet is low in fat since toucans tend to be at risk from athereosclerosis. Does not behave well with fellow species or small birds, particularly at feeding dishes.

CAGE LIFE Inquisitive and calm. Loves to bathe, and frequently. Unable to mimic the human voice. Likes high aviary and needs thick perches about 2½ inches (6cm) for sitting and sleeping. Lays 2 to 4 eggs, incubation 19 to 20 days, fledging 48 to 50 days.

STATUS IN WILD Not listed as endangered.

Cuvier's toucan

Toco Toucan

Ramphistidae toco
ORDER Piciformes FAMILY Ramphastidae

DESCRIPTION 22 inches (55cm). Distinguishing feature is large beak, about a quarter of the total body length; it appears weighty, but is actually light thanks to its honeycombed cell construction. Lacks 'beard' feathers around beak and feathers around eye, and has long tongue frayed at the edges. Wings are short and, like tail, rounded. Walks poorly because first and fourth toes are backwards facing.

NATURAL DISTRIBUTION Eastern South America, from the Guianas to northern Argentina.

HABITAT Tropical rain forests.

DIET Fresh and dried fruit, with some coarse insectivorous food.

SPECIAL NEEDS Be sure diet is low in fat since toucans tend to be at risk from athereosclerosis. Does not behave well with fellow species or small birds, particularly at feeding dishes.

CAGE LIFE Popular bird, requiring care and management similar to that of Cuvier's toucan

STATUS IN WILD Not listed as endangered.

Toco toucan

Hyacinth Macaw

Anodorhynchus hyacinthinus
ORDER Psittaciformes FAMILY Psittacidae

DESCRIPTION 39½ inches (100cm), the largest living parrot, now rare and expensive. Body deep blue-purple accented by yellow eye ring and bold yellow along mandible bottom. Greyish beak exceptionally strong, able to exert 300 pounds (136kg) of biting pressure per square inch. Female usually smaller.

NATURAL DISTRIBUTION Central and southern Brazil, western Bolivia and northeast Paraguay.

HABITAT Highlands, in palm forests, near rivers and lakes, in swamps, usually in pairs or small family groups.

DIET Palm nuts, fruit and snails, also sunflower seed kernels, corn ears and fruit, occasionally a bone and cooked meat.

SPECIAL NEEDS Particularly strong cage or aviary; climbing tree if in house. Replace perches regularly. Do not keep on chain or ring.

CAGE LIFE When screeches, circles overhead with tail streaming, then settles in treetops. Especially close pair bonding and tame with trusted people. Lays 2 to 3 eggs, incubation 28 days, fledging 100 to 120 days.

STATUS IN WILD Appendix 1.

Hyacinth macaw

Green-Winged Macaw

MARRON MACAW
Ara chloroptera
ORDER Psittaciformes FAMILY Psittacidae

DESCRIPTION 33½ to 36 inches (85 to 90cm). Dark red head with green shoulder coverts and large upperwing. Blue wings, rump, uppertail coverts and tail tip. Naked cheeks with red lines, upper mandible pale with greyish on sides. Eyes yellow, legs charcoal. Female smaller. Immatures have dark eyes.

NATURAL DISTRIBUTION Eastern Panama over much of northern South America to Bolivia, Paraguay and northern Argentina.

HABITAT Hilly country and virgin forest, in pairs or small groups. Nests in tree hollows and broken palm trunks.

DIET Parrot food with fruit, greenstuff, sunflower seed kernels, fresh corn and nuts, such as brazils.

SPECIAL NEEDS Bills can be devastating to woodwork, so provide branches as distraction.

CAGE LIFE Quiet, tame, intelligent, kind to children and other pets, but easily frightened by noises and motion. When excited, bare facial area reddens in response to blood flow. Large, strong cage and parrot stand as a free perch when kept in the house. Aviary in the garden with heatable interior room. Provide fresh branches. Close pair bonding. Lays 2 to 3 eggs, incubation 24 to 28 days, fledging 95 days.

STATUS IN WILD Appendix 2.

Green-winged macaw

Great Palm Cockatoo

Probosciger aterrimus
ORDER Psittaciformes FAMILY Psittacidae

DESCRIPTION 19½ to 24 inches (50 to 60cm), largest of all cockatoos. Greyish-black, almost purplish, with bare red facial patch and tongue (with black tip), elongated upper mandible and ragged crest. Eyes brown, beak and legs charcoal. Female smaller with smaller patch.

NATURAL DISTRIBUTION Northeastern Australia and New Guinea and surrounding islands.

HABITAT Tropical and monsoon rain forest bordering on savannah, in lowlands up to 2,500 feet (750m), in small flocks. Nest built in steeply sloping tree cavity, which is used year after year.

DIET Even tiny seeds (in addition to nuts and seeds of pandonus palms) are taken, usually a few at a time, and put in a cavity of the lower mandible; one by one these seeds will be pushed, by the tongue, to the chisel edge of the lower mandible to be broken.

SPECIAL NEEDS Aviary of sturdy materials to protect it from the bird's strong beak.

CAGE LIFE Usually gentle, but noted for dramatic displays as pairs choose territories for breeding, from August to February: male grips stick with foot and drums on trunk. Uses hollow trunks or nest boxes 59¼ inches (150cm) high and 15¾ inches (40cm) in diameter, with 6-inch (15-cm) layer of materials (chewed twigs), placed by both partners. Lays one egg, incubation 33 days by female.

STATUS IN WILD Appendix 1.

Great palm cockatoo

Rose-Breasted Cockatoo

GALAH COCKATOO, ROSEATE COCKATOO
Cacatua roseicappilus
ORDER Psittaciformes   FAMILY Psittacidae

DESCRIPTION 13½ to 15 inches (35 to 38cm), most common cockatoo. Grey above, deep pink below. Low whitish crest, eyes dark brown, pale beak, grey legs. Rare mutation results in absence of melanin from plumage, causing grey areas to be white and feet to be pink. Female's eyes red.

NATURAL DISTRIBUTION Australia and Tasmania.

HABITAT Savannah, open country, eucalyptus woodland, dry interior plains, farmland, parklands and gardens; always inland, follows civilization. In pairs during breeding season, other times in groups. Nests in vertical tree hollows, as well as holes in cliffs. Pairs bond for life and defend nest against intruders. Newly fledged birds gather in treetop nurseries of up to 100 birds, awaiting their parents and the delivery of food. Young spend their first two or three years among large wandering flocks of non-breeding birds. The species has benefited from European settlement, increasing its range and numbers in response to forest clearance and crop planting. Considered a pest by cereal growers.

DIET Parrot mix, cereal seeds, fruit, greenstuff, sunflower seeds, oats, wheat, millet, grass seeds and insects.

SPECIAL NEEDS For best breeding, moisten nest boxes regularly. Avoid diet based on sunflower and other oily seeds, which can lead to fatty tumours.

CAGE LIFE Gentle, playful, intelligent and a good talker with loud voice. Compatible with other large species in aviary, or large metal cage with unheated sheltered area. Leaves and twigs carried into nest box, 20 × 20 × 40 inches (51 × 52 × 102cm), entrance 3½ inches (9cm). Lays 3 to 5 white eggs, incubation 24 to 26 days by both partners, fledging 50 days, still fed and preened another 4 to 5 weeks. Two broods per season common.

STATUS IN WILD Not listed as endangered.

Rose-breasted cockatoo

INDEX

128

CARING FOR EXOTIC BIRDS

ACKNOWLEDGEMENTS

2 Frank S Balthis. 6 Ro-ma Stock/Robert Marien. 8 Ro-ma Stock/Robert Marien. 9bl Duane Patten. 9tr Andrew Rakocz. 9br Norvia Behling. 101 Gregory K Scott. 10r Zoological Society of Philadelphia. 11tr, 11tl Unicorn Stock Photos/Jim Shippee. 11b Norvia Behling. 12l Charlie Heidecker. 12r Duane Patten. 13tl Frank S Balthus. 13br Unicorn Stock Photo/Jim Shippee. 14 Steve Bentsen 15r Unicorn Stock Photos/C Boylan. 17t Gordon Groene. 17b Ro-ma Stock/Robert Marien. 18t Zoological Society of Philadelphia. 18bl Gregory K Scott. 18b4 Norvia Behling. 19 Unicorn Stock Photos/Daniel J Olsen. 20t Diane Calkins. 20b Rosemary Shelton. 21r Margaret Mead. 22 Unicorn Stock Photos/Russel R Grundke. 23 Charlie Heidecker. 24t Erika Klass.

24b Ro-ma Stock/Robert Marien. 25tl Gregory K Scott. 25br Norbert Fischer. 26 Diane Calkins. 27t Ro-ma Stock Photos/Robert Marien. 27b Gregory K Scott. 28 Gregory K Scott. 29 Unicorn Stock Photos/Betts Anderson. 30 Lee and Palmer Paisl. 34 Gregory K Scott. 35 Photri inc. 36 Dennis Avon. 37–38 Eric and David Hosking. 39–40 Dennis Avon. 41 Photri inc/Fritz Prenzel. 42 Dennis Avon. 43 Animal Environments. 44 Joe McDonald. 45 Diane Calkins/Click. 46 Richard Day. 47 Zoological Society of Philadelphia. 48 Charlie Heidecker. 49 Unicorn Stock Photos/Dave Lyons. 50 Photri inc. 51–52 Animal Environments. 53 Frank W Lane. 54 Norvia Behling. 55 Unicorn Stock Photos/Dave Lyons. 56 Frank W Lane. 57 Gregory K Scott. 58 Dennis Avon. 59 Richard Day. 60 Dennis Avon. 61 Eric and

David Hosking. 62 Zoological Society of Philadelphia. 63 Rosemary Shelton. 64 Rubin Klass. 65 Bob Yellen. 66 Gregory K Scott. 67 Charlie Heidecker. 68 Richard Day. 69 Unicorn Stock Photos/Wayne Flloyd. 70 Photonats/Gay Bumgarner. 71 Frank L Balthus. 72 Photri inc. 73 Gregory K Scott. 74 Norvia Behling. 75 Photri inc. 76 Photri inc. 77 Charlie Heidecker. 78 Dennis Avon. 79 Gregory K Scott. 80–81 Eric and David Hosking. 82–85 Dennis Avon. 86 Eric and David Hosking. 87 Photri inc. 88 Eric and David Hosking. 89 Dennis Avon. 90 Eric and David Hosking. 91 Dennis Avon. 92 Eric and David Hosking. 93 Photri inc/Kamal. 94 Eric and David Hosking. 95 Dennis Avon. 95 Gregory K Scott. 97 Frank W Lane. 98 John Edwards. 99 Leonard Lee Rue III. 100 Eric and David

Hosking. 101 John Edwards. 102 Rosemary Shelton. 103 Buffalo Zoo. 104 Frank W Lane. 105 Eric and David Hosking. 106 Richard Day. 107 Gregory K Scott. 108–109 Frank W Lane. 110 Dennis Avon. 111 John Edwards. 112 John Edwards/Denver Zoo. 113 Dennis Avon. 114 Milton Heiberg. 115 Brooke Morrison. 116 Buffalo Zoological Gardens. 117 John Edwards/Denver Zoo. 118–119 Eric and David Hosking. 120 Brooke Morrison. 121 Frank L Balthis. 122 Jungle Talk Parrot Productions. 123 Unicorn Stock Photos/Russel R Grundke. 124 Ro-ma Stock/Robert Marien.

r = right, l = left, t = top, b = bottom